State and Religion in China

State and Religion in China

Historical and Textual Perspectives

ANTHONY C. YU

OPEN COURT
Chicago and La Salle, Illinois

This book has been reproduced in a print-on-demand format from the 2005 Open Court printing.

To order books from Open Court, call 1-800-815-2280 or visit www.opencourtbooks.com.

Open Court Publishing Company is a division of Carus Publishing Company.

Library of Congress Cataloging-in-Publication Data

Yu, Anthony C., 1938–
    State and religion in China : historical and textual perspectives / Anthony C. Yu.
        p. cm.
Includes bibliographical references and index.
    ISBN 0-8126-9552-6 (alk. paper)
    1. Religion and state—China. 2. China—Religion. I. Title.
    BL65.S8Y82 2004
    322'.1'0951—dc22

                                        2004024762

This book includes the revised and expanded text of a lecture sponsored by the Institute for World Religions and the Pacific School of Religions at Berkeley, California.

For

Waitong and Sophie Tang
and
Patrick and Lucia Yu

所親以立宗廟
蓋建威
銷萌
一民
之至權也

We make it a point to establish personally our ancestral temple,
because this is the ultimate power to build up our authority,
eliminate the sprouts of rebellion, and make the people one.

—Emperor Yuandi 元 帝 (r. 48–32 B.C.E.) of the Han

The plain working truth is that it is not only good for people to be shocked
occasionally, but absolutely necessary to the progress of society that they
should be shocked pretty often. But it is not good for people to be garotted
occasionally, or at all. That is why it is a mistake to treat an atheist as you treat
a garotter, or to put "bad taste" on the footing of theft and murder. The need
for freedom of evolution is the sole basis of toleration, the sole valid argument
against Inquisitions and Censorships, the sole reason for not burning heretics
and sending every eccentric person to the madhouse.

In short, our ideals, like the gods of old, are constantly demanding human
sacrifices.

—Bernard Shaw, *The Quintessence of Ibsenism*

CONTENTS

PREFACE

THIS BOOK IS A MUCH EXPANDED version of "On State and Religion in China: A Brief Historical Reflection," delivered at the Pacific School of Religion in Berkeley in the autumn of 2002 as the third of the annual Venerable Master Hsüan Hua Memorial Lectures, cosponsored by the Institute for World Religions and the Graduate Theological Union. It was then published in *Religion East and West* 3 (June 2003), pp. 1–20. For that publication, I owe Professor David Keightley a large debt of careful reading and criticism. Although a considerable amount of material has since been added to the essay, the subject itself merits an even larger treatment, but contractual limitation of time has necessarily moderated the length and scope of the study.

I wish to thank my generous hosts from both the Institute and the Theological Union for a memorable visit on the occasion of the lecture. Professor Henry Rosemont, friend and colleague for almost three decades, has provided steadfast encouragement and stimulating critique, without which the study might not have come to birth at all. Professors Robert Campany, Tom Michael, and Zhou Yiqun have all offered the kind of meticulous correction and commentary that only true friends are wont to provide. Their generous efforts have vastly improved the book, but I alone am responsible for lingering faults and failings. A word of heartfelt gratitude is due Dr. Yuan Zhou, Curator of the East Asian Library, Mr. Eizaburo Okuizumi, Japanese Librarian, and Mr. Qian Xiaowen, Assistant to the Curator, The University of Chicago, for their unfailing assistance in the location and acquisition of needed materials. Mr. Dongfeng Xu, doctoral candidate in Comparative Literature at the University of Chicago, kindly helped prepare the Index.

QTW   *Quan Tang wen* 全唐文 (5 vols. fasc. of 1814 text. Shanghai: Guji, 1990).

SBBY   *Sibu beiyao* 四部備要

SBCK   *Sibu congkan* 四部叢刊

T.   *Taishō shinshū dai-zōkyō* (The Tripiṭaka) 大正新脩大藏經, 85 vols. Eds. Takakusu Junjirō 高楠順次郎 and Watanabe Kaikyoku 渡邉海旭 (Tokyo: Daizō shuppan kabushiki gaisha, 1924–32).

THY   *Tang hui yao* 唐會要, comp. and ed., Wang Pu 王溥 (3 vols. Beijing: Zhonghua shuju, 1955 [1992 printing]).

References to all Standard Histories, unless otherwise indicated, are taken from the Kaiming edition of *Ershiwu shi* 二十五史 (1934; rpt. Taipei: Kaiming Shudian, 1959).

ABBREVIATIONS

CHAC *The Cambridge History of Ancient China: From the Origins of Civilization to 221 B.C.*, Michael Loewe and Edward L. Shaughnessy, eds. (Cambridge: Cambridge University Press, 1999).

CHC *The Cambridge History of China, Vol. 1, The Ch'in and Han Empires 221 B.C.–A.D. 220.*, Denis Twitchett and Michael Loewe, eds. (Cambridge: Cambridge University Press, 1986). *Vol. 3, Part 1, Sui and T'ang China 589–906*, Denis Twitchett, ed. (Cambridge: Cambridge University Press, 1979).

CLEAR *Chinese Literature: Essays Articles Reviews*

CQ *China Quarterly*

DZ *Zhengtong Daozang* 正統道藏

HJAS *Harvard Journal of Asiatic Studies*

HR *History of Religions*

JAS *Journal of Asian Studies*

Legge James Legge, trans., *The Chinese Classics* (5 vols. Rpt. of Oxford University Press editions. Taibei: Wenshizhe chubanshe, 1972)

QQHS *Quan shanggu sandai Qin Han Sanguo Liuchao wen* 全上古三代秦漢三國六朝文, compiled by Yan Kejun 嚴可均 (5 vols. Shanghai: Zhonghua, 1965).

1

Introduction: The Thesis

IN THE COMPLEX AND THORNY RELATIONS between Western
nations and China, one contentious issue that has received
persistent attention concerns religion and its treatment
by the government of China. On the side of the People's
Republic, there is little ambiguity regarding its attitude
towards religion and the role of the state in its control and
governance. The Chinese Constitution adopted in 1954 ex-
pressly guarantees all citizens the freedom of both religious
belief and "unbelief." The edited version of the famous
"Document 19" published by the official Party journal, *Red
Flag*, on June 16th, 1982, provides a brief but illuminating
account of the Party's understanding of religion and also a
succinct statement of government policy on religion. "Religion," it tells us, "is a historical phenomenon pertaining to
a definite period in the development of human society. It
has its own cycle of emergence, development, and demise."
Insofar as this phenomenon has existed in time, "the
earliest mentality reflected the low level of production and
the sense of awe toward natural phenomena of primitive
peoples."[1]

This recognition provides a Communist state like
China, committed as it is to a firm avowal of atheism, the
justification to tolerate and accommodate the existence of
religion. "The political power in a Socialist state can in no
way be used to promote any one religion," the Document
declares, "nor can it be used to forbid any one religion, as
long as it is only a question of *normal* religious beliefs and
practices."[2] On the other hand, the establishment of the
PRC had meant for the ruling Communist Party a determined commitment to rid China's religious traditions and
communities of their "erroneous" ties to the "feudal" past

and completely sever them from any link to colonial or imperialistic structures of governance from abroad. Religion, if it is to exist within such a nation, must fulfill the state-mandated obligation of being "patriotic," in the sense that religion would never, in Document 19's words, "be permitted to make use in any way of religious pretexts to oppose the Party's leadership or the Socialist system, or to destroy national or ethnic unity."[3] If religion is permited to exist under these terms, it does not mean, however, that its future or flourishing is thereby guaranteed. With greater social, economic, and educational developments such as those advocated and instituted by Socialism and Communism, the document confidently asserts that "religion will eventually disappear from human history."[4]

When we turn to the Western reaction and assessment of China on this issue, the representation is equally unambiguous. The crucial paragraph printed in the "Country Reports on Human Rights Practices—2001" released by the U.S. Department of State in March, 2002, notices how "unapproved religious groups . . . continued to experience varying degrees of official interference, harrassment, and repression," and it proceeds to rehearse duly different examples of such repressive activities with respect to Christian churches, the Tibetan community loyal to the Dalai Lama, and forced relocation "of thousands of Tibetan Buddhist nuns and monks from the Serthar Tibetan Buddhist Institute in western Sichuan Province."[5] Echoing the report, occasional accounts of the Government's treatment of the Falun Gong adherents, the arrest of dissenting Catholic prelates and sectarian Protestant activities (for example, unauthorized dissemination of printed Bibles and Christian writings), and the destruction of religious buildings such as Christian churches have appeared regularly in the past years in *The New York Times*, the *Washington Post*, and other news media.

Does the current situation mean that a conflictive impasse in the interpretation of Chinese policy on religion is unavoidable and unresolvable? In reflecting upon such a question and its implications, I am immediately reminded of the frequent protests by various Chinese leaders and elite personnel to the effect that the West lacks adequate knowledge of China. An example of this gesture can be found in the words of former President Jiang Zemin, who said in an interview with *The New York Times* in 2001: "I hope that the Western world can understand China better."[6] Although in context Jiang was not addressing directly the topic of religion but a whole range of issues on economic development, human rights, and relations with Taiwan and Tibet, his remark provides a measure of incentive for a concerned student of both religion and Chinese civilization like myself to take up the problem, however modestly. The aim of this brief study, however, is not so much an attempt to justify the Chinese leader or his followers in defense of their policies as it is to assist an academic and lay readership in grasping the historical lineage of certain governmental policies toward religion. The thesis I hope to argue is simple: that there has never been a period in China's historical past in which the government of the state, in imperial and post-imperial form, has pursued a neutral policy toward religion, let alone encouraged, in terms dear to American idealism, its "free exercise." The impetus to engage religion, on the part of the central government, stems first of all from its own subscription to a specific form of religiosity that, most appropriately, should be named a state religion. For more than two millennia, the core ideological convictions shaping and buttressing imperial governance also direct correlatively the purpose and process to regulate, control, and exploit all rivalling religious traditions whenever it is deemed feasible and beneficial to the state.

So stated, the thesis is not exactly novel or original. In

Religion in Chinese Society, a pioneering study published almost half a century ago, C.K. Yang had already observed unerringly that, among the three major civilizations of Europe, India, and China, "the role of religion in political life has been the least systematically studied" in the last variety.[7] Building on the threefold typology formulated by Joachim Wach on how a religion could serve as an ally of the state, renounce secular participation and withdraw into seclusion, or seek greater political gains (preservation, recognition, or independence) by opposing state power, Yang's book, intended to redress the lack, further asserts that "in recent Chinese religious life, all these forms were simultaneously present to some degree."[8] The argument I want to add is that these forms of interaction with state power need not be confined to recent history, nor should it be averred that the policy of stringent and systematic state intervention in religious life has been implemented only recently by the Chinese Communists. The motivation to promote, regulate, coopt, and control religion, as a recent work of Chinese scholarship has also sought to demonstrate,[9] had already taken shape in China's high antiquity. The substantiation of my thesis thus focuses on the earlier periods of Chinese history down to the Tang.

2

Defining Religion in Chinese:
The Detour of "A Term Question"

THE THESIS FORMULATED IN THE PREVIOUS CHAPTER may seem to run counter to some part of scholarly opinion on historical Chinese culture, especially on the contentious issue on how to locate, analyze, and understand in that culture different data or phenomena that seem to embody or manifest religiosity, however defined. Part of the recent controversy of scholarship, moreover, extends to the discussion of the modern term for religion in Chinese (*zongjiao* 宗教), one of the many neologisms allegedly coined by the Japanese in the nineteenth century and re-imported for Chinese usage,[1] and whether such a term is applicable to cultural phenomena of early or imperial China. Even if it is, so the question continues, is it a proper or adequate synonym of the word "religion" in its full English and European linguistic connotations? This alleged lack of clarity and consensus on a definition of religion for the Chinese involving the Chinese language itself makes for considerable difficulty not merely in the analysis of the subject within the culture of any pre-modern period; it may provoke astonishment and even resistance if one were to assert that the central government of pre-imperial and imperial China was founded squarely on religious premises. A modern Chinese historian is not atypical in his sweeping judgment when he asserts that fundamentally speaking, China has no religion as such (*Zhongguo genben meiyou zongjiao* 中國根本沒有宗教).[2] To the student of the modern history of interpreting Chinese "religion(s)," such an extreme opinion, itself more revelatory of this particular scholar's preference for a secularistic interpretation of Chinese culture than of understanding religion itself, hardly astonishes, for it may be said to echo opinions handed down for centuries by both foreign and native scholarship. Following either consciously or unwittingly the yardstick of a re-defined Confucianism proposed by Matteo Ricci's theological apologetics, European savants of the nineteenth (for instance Wilhelm Grube)[3] and twentieth centuries have long argued that most aspects of traditional China's society are essentially secular. Hence the ringing declaration of Max Weber:

> The Confucian had no desire to be "saved" either from the migration of souls or from punishment in the beyond. Both ideas were unknown to Confucianism. The Confucian wished neither for salvation from life, which was affirmed, nor salvation from the social world, which was accepted as given. He thought of prudently mastering the opportunities of this world through self-control. He desired neither to be saved from evil nor from a fall of man, which he knew not. He desired to be saved from nothing except perhaps the undignified barbarisms of social rudeness. Only the infraction of piety, the one basic social duty, could constitute "sin" for the Confucian.[4]

Even the late Joseph Needham, who certainly cannot be accused of either a lack of interest in the subject or ignorance of religion's multifarious aspects and manifestations in traditional China, may stumble on this issue. While acknowledging "some relation between aspiring monumentality in stone and the influences of mystical religion" when elaborating on traditional architecture and civil engineering, he nonetheless can claim that "the Chinese mood was essentially secular, loving life and Nature. Hence the gods had to conform, to sit and be worshipped in buildings identical with the halls of families and palaces, or not to be worshipped at all."[5]

This remark of Needham's about the deities having "to conform, to sit and be worshipped in buildings identical with the halls and palaces," reveals unwittingly his own theory of religion, his undeclared assumption about what does or does not count as a fitting site for worship in a Chinese context. Despite his long years of loving labor devoted to the study of China, the eminent historian of Chinese science could not quite understand that there is no self-evident and universal norm for linking place and sacrality. Neither the gothic spires of Chartres or Westminster nor the upturned eaves of the Shaolin Monastery need locate authentic religiosity for the Chinese. In this light, the scholarly biases of using official state-sponsored Confucianism to represent the cultural tenor of the entire society and Christianity to determine whether Confucianism should be considered a religion, ironically, have been abetted by the recent discussion on linguistic matters as well.

As has been mentioned previously, the modern Japanese term for religion, *shūkyō*, was invented in the early Meiji period by the deliberate combination of the two Kanji characters *zong* (宗) and *jiao* (教). Since its appropriation for Chinese usage by such late imperial figures as Huang Zunxian 黃遵憲 (1848–1905), an Administrative Aide of the Qing's Diplomatic Legation posted to Japan in 1877–82, and Liang Qichao 梁啟超 (1873–1929), the reformer historian and scholar, the term has soon become the accepted standard designation of religion.[6] Usage, however, only stirs up frequent puzzlement and controversy, for few Sinological scholars to this day seem able to agree on what is the exact meaning of the neologism or to offer an acceptable etymology for its definition. The most extreme position in this discussion is that because the term was supposedly coined in the modern period, and in a foreign land to boot, it would be an unfit reference to any pre-modern Chinese cultural phenomenon. The more moderate view would argue whether, even if the term *zongjiao* is allowed to tag Daoism and Buddhism flourishing in historical China, it could be used also for naming Confucianism, especially when one character (*jiao*) making up the composite term has served as the pride of nomenclature for this particular tradition's didactic mission and content. Already in the time of Matteo Ricci (1552–1610) and Michele Ruggieri (1543–1607), the efforts of these Jesuit missionaries to China during the late Ming were marked by their arduous but ingenious apologetic move to dissociate in the mind of the elite Chinese the Three Religions (*san jiao*) of their native society from the "orthodox religion of the Lord of Heaven [*Tianzhu zhengjiao* 天主正教]" that the Europeans were said to have brought from the West.[7]

Despite Ricci's efforts, ironically, what complicated the discourse on Chinese culture and society of the last two centuries by both native and foreign writers has been, of course, the long shadow cast by a religion like Christianity that, whenever the Chinese term *zongjiao* is used, almost inevitably becomes its assumed standard referent. A great part of the debate on whether Confucianism as both transmitted doctrines and diffused institutions may be said to take on a "religious" character frequently turns on the implicit or explicit comparison of the tradition with some aspect or version of Christianity. Tellingly, for example, Wing-tsit Chan's modern critique of the late imperial and early Republican attempt, on the part of the reformer Kang Youwei 康有為 (1858–1927) and followers, to canonize Confucianism as a "national religion" after the demise of the Qing imperial government is based on his conviction that such advocates "do not prove that Confucianism is a religion, certainly not a religion *in the Western sense* of an organized church comparable to Buddhism or Taoism."[8] Because my study intends to demonstrate that forms of religious life and practice were inextricably bound up with state policies and power from the earliest stage of China's recorded history, a brief exmination of the possible linguistic genealogies of the term *zong-*

jiao itself may help to elucidate and advance my argument.

If, then, this term for religion was coined during the early Meiji period, the additional questions to be raised in this regard ought to be: what was the historical necessity that led to its invention and what might be the underlying linguistic and textual reasons for the choice of the two Kanji characters? Japanese scholarship (of which this study can mention only the most pertinent items here) which has examined these questions traces the context to the year 1869 (Meiji 2), when the Japanese government was negotiating with European powers for a treaty of commerce that would also permit the foreigners to engage in religious activities. The Japanese had to find a word to translate the German *Religionsübung* (religious practice), and *zongjiao* was eventually chosen.[9] According to another study, however, several years of the same decade, in fact, saw Japanese thinkers hard at work in various publications exploring different terminologies built from Kanji to convey the flavor and meaning of the Western term, and some of these included the following : *sōshi* (for the Chinese *zongzhi* 宗旨), *shinkyō* for *shenjiao* 神教, *sōshi hōkyō* for *zongzhifa jiao* 宗旨法教, *seidō* for *shengdao* 聖道, *kyōmon* for *jiaomen* 教門, and the single word, *kyō* for *jiao* 教.[10] A closer look at the semantic implications derived from Chinese sources that the Japanese might have read can shed important light on the two Chinese words eventually chosen.

For the graph *zong* 宗, the primary nominal meaning as ancestor, the ancestral lineage, and the ancestral temple itself would extend the denomination to the appointed official (i.e., the Da zongbo 大宗伯) in charge of the most important sacrifices (alleged to be established in the Zhou) to be offered to the pantheon of deities and imperial ancestors.[11] This complex of associations seems to have spawned also the verbal meaning of *zun* 尊, to honor, revere, and obey. From the nominal meaning comes as well the notion of root, origin, and basis (*gen* 根, *ben* 本). A further development is the idea of tracking something to its source, purpose, or first principle (e.g., 追宗) or the verbal sense of elevating/exalting (for example, *zong yang* 宗仰) a person or a concept to its fundamental or ultimate significance.[12] The latter shades of meaning, it should be pointed out, seem to have developed from a discourse pointedly at odds with the Confucian one, for that tradition's subscription to, and support of, the ideology of state cult has been consistently built on a vocabulary intimately connected to ancestral reverence and clan ethics.[13] In the writings of the early Daoist thinkers, on the other hand, there was already an unmistakable attempt to dissociate the word *zong* from the circuit of human kinship and kingship structures and re-locate it in the context of impersonal phenomena. The singular occurence of the word in Chapter 70 of the *Laozi* already hints at this move by displacing the kinship and rulership connotations of the terms *zong* and *jun*: "Words have an original purpose/principle (*zong*), and activities have a basis (*jun*) 言有宗, 事有君."[14]

The most prominent development of this tendency, however, is discernible in a text like the *Zhuangzi*. The familiar title of Chapter 6 (*da zongshi* 大宗師), translated by A.C. Graham as "The teacher who is the ultimate ancestor,"[15] can actually and more aptly be rendered as "The Teacher of the Great/First Principle," because this very chapter accentuates the irrelevance of human kinship for understanding how the cosmic Dao operates. Even more pointed are such observations scattered throughout the book.

Chapter 5, "De chong fu 德充符": "[Wang Tai] names on his own the transformation of things and holds fast to their principles 命物之化而守其宗也."

Chapter 13, "Tian Dao 天道": "As for the understanding [found] in the virtue of Heaven and Earth, this is called the great origin and great principle 夫明白於天地之德者, 此之謂

大本大宗"; and "as for the virtue of the sovereign and king, it takes Heaven and Earth to be its first principle 夫帝王之德, 以天地為宗."[16]

Chapter 33, "Tianxia 天下 ": "He who has not left his first principle is called a Heavenly Person . . . . He who uses Heaven as his first principle, virtue as his origin, the Way as his gate, and who becomes prescient through changes and transformations is called a sage 不離於宗, 謂之天人 . . . . 以天為宗, 以德為本, 以道為門, 兆於變化, 謂之聖人."[17]

This variant range of meanings would especially fund the semantics of Buddhist usage of the word after the religion's penetration into China. Not only is the word chosen to indicate a particular divisional lineage of the religion (for instance, *Tiantai zong*; and *Maoshan zong* for the Daoist tradition), but Buddhist writings also employ it to refer to the Sanskrit term *siddhānta*, meaning principal doctrine, proposition, axiom, dogma, an established conclusion, and an authoritative text.[18] Relative to the Buddha himself, the term is often translated and also transcribed as *xitan* 悉檀 in Chinese, pointing to the four modes of the Patriarch's teachings, the last of which being the perfect and highest truth. Because of this assocation with both native religious practices (ancestor worship as both royal and clan religion that we shall discuss below) and Buddhism, the connotation of the word *zong* in the compound *zongjiao* should not be difficult to imagine.

Investigation into medieval Chinese texts can reveal some astonishing aspects of the use of this term in the history of its devolution in pre-modern China. An initial search through a small part of the database of the *Wenyuange Siku quanshu dianziban* 文淵閣四庫全書電子版, most recently installed in the library of The University of Chicago, has yielded at least several hundred "hits" of a possible total of several thousands. A preliminary canvassing of the data, apart from a small number of samples that clearly reflects the computer's mechanical misreadings (e.g., the two words *zong* and *jiao* were juxtaposed continguously by pure accident, and a reading of the sense in question quickly demonstrates that they were meant to be separate words belonging to different syntactic units of the same sentence rather than an integral binomial term), has indicated, at least to this reader, that the term appears almost exclusively in texts associated with Buddhism. Indeed, the word in many places seems verily a synonym of Buddhism.

One very early example of *zongjiao* as neologism in the Chinese language may be found in a formal reply (among twenty-six named officials) by an official named Yuan Ang 袁昂 at the time of the Liang Emperor Wudi (502–47), who solicited among his courtiers reasoned refutations of the famous polemic against Buddhism in the treatise, "On Destruction of the Soul (*Shenmie lun* 神滅論)," authored by the Confucian official Fan Zhen 范縝. The pertinent passage in Yuan's letter to the monk-official Fayun 法雲 issuing the imperial request reads (in my tentative translation):

> I have reverently searched through the holy texts, and they indeed plainly speak of negativity and non-being. But in response to *zongjiao*, we may turn to and rely on what is actually there. In accordance with being we may talk of being, but we still may not be able to exhaust nature. Thus on the basis of negativity and non-being, we may discuss non-being. In this way we may range very far 仰尋聖典，既顯言不無，但應宗教，歸依其有。就有談有，猶未能盡性，遂於不無論無，斯可遠矣.[19]

Even if the entire passage at the moment eludes a completely accurate rendering, the meaning of the term *zongjiao* in such a context seems comprehensible as either "the revered teaching/religion" or "the teaching/religion that has an ultimate basis or principle" (that is, 有所宗仰的教 in modern vernacular Chinese). Another textual example, validating this line of conjecture, may be found in a collection of miscellany on various topics dated to the Jianyan 建炎 (1127–1131) through the Deyou 德祐 (1275–76) periods of the Song. Here the term's meaning, with an explicit qualifier, seems much more straightforward: "As our territorial space is divided in the middle, even so the revered teaching/religion (*zongjiao*) of the Buddhists is also set apart as North and South, in such a way that each [division] honors its own masters and teaches its own way 區宇中分，而釋氏宗教亦判為南北，各師其師，各道其道."[20] A third example of the evolving intimacy between *zong* and *jiao* that sheds light on both its individual meanings can be found in the introductory encomium of the medieval *Transformation Text on The Subduing of Demons* 降魔變文. "After [the Tang Emperor Xuanzong] had brought about appropriate cultural transformations of his domain," the text says, "he often extolled the Three Religions (*sanjiao* 三教). Sometimes he would probe and search Confucianism and Daoism in the exhaustive quest for nature and origin. In annotating and explicating Buddhism's highest principles, his sentences would be as profound as they are far-reaching 或以探尋儒道，盡性窮原。注解釋宗，句深相遠."[21]

In the early Zen classic on religous genealogy, *The Transmission of the Lamp of the Jingde Period* (compiled in 1004), we have yet another striking appearance of the binomial term *zongjiao* itself in one of the narrative episodes. Replying to the ninth of ten queries posed by a certain Recluse Shi, the particular question examining why the Buddha did not transmit his message to all people but limited it only to a single disciple, the Chan Master Zongmi said, "After the Buddha passed away, it was entrusted to Kāśyapa as an individual to take turn in assuming successive transmission thereafter. This refers generally to how the current generation can be the revered teaching/religion's lord (*zong jiao zhu*) 此亦蓋論當代為宗教主."[22] I have segregated the romanization of the Chinese term, because an alternative reading can make the sentence read: "this refers generally to how the current generation can honor or adhere to (reading *zong* as a verb) the lord/founder of the teaching/religion (*jiao zhu*)," but the second reading seems a bit forced, since it turns the full verb *wei* into only an auxiliary verb.

Finally, another example is traceable to another famous Zen Buddhist text of the Song, the *Wudeng huiyuan* 五燈會元, authored by the monk Puji 普濟. In *juan* 10, a passage reads: "The monk requested the master to ascend his ritual seat, and when the crowd had all gathered, he then invited him to lift up and proclaim the revered religion/teaching (*zongjia*) 僧問師登寶座, 大眾咸臻, 便請舉揚宗教."[23]

However the semantic issue is to be finally resolved, the appearance of the term *zongjiao* in so many texts before the nineteenth century (and I have cited only a handful from a sum of possibly several hundred instances) is arresting, to say the least. If they had seen any or all of them, the Japanese writers of the nineteenth century should be credited with aptitude and wisdom in selecting this binome for their use. From the examples we have cited, however, it seems obvious as well that the binomial term in these medieval texts is used as a metaphor for the Buddhist religion and not as a generic equivalent for the Western word, religion. In borrowing this term to translate the German term for "religious practice," the Japanese had certainly invested it with meaning that it might not have possessed in the prior Chinese context. We should not forget that the term emerging possibly in the sixth century and then appropriated for further use by another culture in the nineteenth has always been a linguistic artifact fashioned out of Chinese characters or Kanji for the designation of a cultural phenomenon we now call "religion" or a variety thereof. The term betokens an act of language, a deliberate selection of a metaphor that is in turn part of a larger discourse *of* and *on* "religion."[24] Moreover, regardless of whether this term had been generated from the Chinese language of the sixth century or the nineteenth, the binome, we should notice, had been produced from a context inextricably tied to cultural otherness, to encounter with "religion" involving non-native cultures. The Japanese appropriation of it in the nineteenth century was motivated precisely by the need to accommodate the mention of religion during the process of confrontation and negotiation with foreign imperialism. The Chinese importation of this term back to their native land were apparently oblivious to its evolved significance in their own history. Far from being a creation of alien traditions in modernity, *zongjiao* in its historical deployment had been itself fashioned by an alien religion negotiating its way into China. As such, the term has received discursive embodiment in Chinese religious texts for centuries; strictly speaking, it was not "invented" by the Japanese in the nineteenth century like scientific terms in Chinese words or Kanji have to be invented *de novo* to translate chemical elements from the periodic table.

Returning to the native dimension of our brief detour, the semantic field of the singular word *jiao* itself in classical Chinese texts seems to combine the transmission of knowledge with authoritative instruction, in such a way that both content and action of the process (as noun or verb) are expected to modify affective orientation and behavior. Understandably, therefore, the word (frequently indicated by a shift of tone in poetry and prose from the departing tone of the *xiao* 效 rhyme scheme to the level tone of the *yao* 肴 rhyme scheme according to later rhyming dictionaries) acquires early the added meaning of causality, in the sense that such and such a factor or agent will cause someone to do something or something to happen.[25] Of the early extant Confucian documents, the *Analects* records only seven instances of usage of the term in the text, but the number jumps to thirty-four in the *Mencius*. In a crucial passage on the posited legacy of education—its alleged purpose and content—inherited from the revered dynasties of Xia, Yin (Shang), and Zhou, Mencius resorts to phonetic glosses or punning definitions pervasively favored by ancient thinkers to make his point:

> *Xiang* 庠, *xu* 序, *xue* 學, and *xiao* 校 were established for the purpose of teaching [the people] (*jiao zhi* 教之). *Xiang* means rearing; *xiao* means teaching; and *xu* means archery. The Xia called it teaching, the Yin called it archery, and the Zhou called it rearing. *Xue* (learning) was a common name in the Three Dynasties, because it was used by all to make the people understand human relationships (*renlun* 人倫). When human relationships are understood by those [in authority] above, the little people below will be affectionate. Should a Kingly One (*wangzhe* 王者) arise, he would certainly take this condition as his model. Therefore, he who practices [such an ideal] will become a mentor to the Kingly One (*wei wangzhe shi* 為王者師).[26]

As can be seen from his remark, Mencius characteristically deploys the oppositional category of "above" and "below," thereby making hierarchical exemplum and mimetic dependence the bedrock of his teaching on ethics and politics. In sharp contrast to what people in the modern societies of East and West may presume, teaching is not strictly a secular affair in the sense of disinterested dissemination of information or transmission of knowledge by public or private institutions. For the ancient Chinese thinker, educative authority is deposited in the rulers, those empowered socially and politically to be authoritarian, in such a way that their subjects will conform to the teachings handed down. "When the Son of Heaven had decreed that there should be instruction," according to the Han compendium *Liji* or *Record of Rites*, "then [the princes] would build the halls of teaching 天子命之教然後為之學."[27]

The institution of teaching and learning, moreover, is presumed to be directly related to the state's "authorized" ability to govern in this manner, as the 143 uses of the word *jiao* in the *Record of Rites* abundantly illustrate. Even if this compendium's content is nothing more than the fantasy of Han bureaucrats, the ideology so systematically articulated as the paradigmatic and binding practice of the ancients is consonant with the convictions of the earlier Confucians, one of which being that the different model dynasties's reputed paideutic success in behavioral modification becomes, as we shall note immediately below, a principal measure of its cultural achievement. Even the tutor of the prince derives his ultimate significance from teaching the person in power, not necessarily the subjects the student happens to govern who may eventually be the alleged beneficiaries of such tutelage. This powerful Mencian passage is undoubtedly the key source to the entry by Xu Shen 許慎 (*ca.* CE 55–*ca.* 149) in the first dictionary he compiled during the Han. Directly echoing Mencius's explanation, Xu glosses the word *jiao* with the following definition: "What those [in authority] above administer, and what those down below emulate 上所施, 下所效也."[28] This peculiar thread of Confucian emphasis is visible more than a thousand years later in the glosses on *jiao* in the Song rhyming lexicon *Guangyun* (compiled by Chen Pengnian 陳彭年, 1st edition CE 1007): "*jiao* is admonition, also imitation. The [*Chunqiu*] *yuanmingbao* says: 'Heaven suspends patterned images and humans act on these things; this is called *jiao* 天垂文象人行其事謂之教'."[29] Even if one were to stretch the interpretation somewhat and construe the last quotation as stressing the importance of human initiative in the perception of celestial signs, it may also be regarded, arguably, as an assertion of natural revelation already firmly encoded in the scheme of things. The proper response to such revelation, repeatedly adumbrated in thinkers from Warring States figures to the Han

Confucian minister Dong Zhongshu 董仲舒 (*ca.* 179–*ca.* 104 B.C.E.), is for alertness and perspicacity in the reading of "texts" surfacing in both culture and nature.

Mencius's reference to the three dynasties of Xia, Yin, and Zhou is symptomatic of the perennial preoccupation, on the part of classical Chinese thinkers, with assessing the legacy of their reputed forebears, usually resulting in naming, as it were, the distinctive "period style" of the respective dynastic culture. From the perspective of modern critical history, the three ancient dynasties might have represented only so many different and isolated tribal traditions, but the tendency of the mid-Zhou (as most discernible in a subject like Confucius himself) and Warring States discourses already sought to emphasize cultural continuity and complementarity. This process might well have generated the term "Three Teachings (*sanjiao* 三教)" that has, in turn, produced considerable discussion in modern scholarship on the history of Chinese religions. In the chapter bearing specifically this term as a title, another Han compendium by the name of *Bohutong* 白虎通 attributed to the historian-official Ban Gu 班固 (32–92) but probably a later text,[30] there can be found a discussion of the principal themes of "education" of the three model dynasties of antiquity. Thus the Xia is said to emphasize loyalty (*zhong* 忠), the Yin reverence (*jing* 敬), and the Zhou culture itself (*wen* 文).[31]

This reference to the *sanjiao* of China's antique culture, as my translation above attempts to show, may not harbor any explicit religious connotation. With the inception of religious Daoism and the arrival of Indian Buddhism in rapid succession and, ironically, at practically the same period posited for the formation of the text of *Bohutong*, the semantic content of the term shifts radically. Henceforth, its preponderant reference has to do with the three major religious traditions of Buddhism (*shi* 釋), Daoism (*dao* 道), and Confucianism (*ru* 儒).[32] Although early medieval texts frequently use a specific adjective coupled with the term *jiao* or the term *dao* to indicate which particular tradition they are treating (for instance, *fojiao* or *shijiao* for Buddhism, *rudao* for Confucianism),[33] the terms "Three Ways (*sandao* 三道)" and "Three Teachings/Religions (*sanjiao* 三教)" soon became the standard collective nomenclatures for the three religions, with the latter, in fact, displacing the former in popularity of usage by the time of the Sui-Tang. In the "Biography of Li Shiqian 李世謙," the grand-nephew of the official Li Ling 李靈 of the Latter Wei (sixth century), the subject of the account "was queried by a visitor on the good and bad of the Three Religions (*sanjiao*). Whereupon Li replied: 'Buddhism is the sun, Daoism the moon, and Confucianism the five planets.' Because he could not stump him, the guest stopped."[34]

It is customary for modern scholars loyal to Confucianism to insist that the term *sanjiao* notwithstanding, the historical Confucians themselves never considered their "teaching" to be a phenomenon equivalent in form and substance to either Daoism or Buddhism. In sum, their argument would run something like this: even if one allows the term *sanjiao* to be rendered as the three religions, Confucianism as a *jiao* cannot be a true parallel to either Daoism or Buddhism as a *jiao*. If pressed for further explanation, the resistance to regard *jiao* as a genus that can help define the three traditions as species usually is based on such factors as the following: (1) that Confucius himself did not orient his teachings to theistic assumptions or the power of transcendent beings; (2) that his teachings offer no clue to afterlife or eschatology; (3) that there is no ecclesiastical organization or priestly cast among Confucian communities; and (4) that there is no insistence on such a ritual as prayer, a practice universally regarded as religious.

Without dwelling on the dispute itself, it may be observed here that the complete tacit endorsement by Confucius of sacrifices to ancestors (both royal and commoner) in ethics and politics has always been, as we shall see below, the linchpin of the enduring state cult ideology down through the centuries. Without a robust conviction on the "afterlife" that manifests itself first and foremost in ancestral intervention and supervenience in human affairs, the imperial cult no less than the ordinary subjects of the Chinese state could not have persisted in their particular forms of historical existence for so long. Scattered throughout the *Record of Rites* is an immense amount of both observations and prescriptions for rituals concerning the disposition of dead kin, burial and mourning, and the regular offering of sacrifices to the deceased ancestors. Although the principal targets of instruction intended by this compendium are the ruler and his ministerial subjects, it is also apparent that the distilled meaning of these rituals, echoing the emphasis of an earlier Confucian classic like the *Xunzi* (Chapter 19 in *juan* 13), is meant to instruct and benefit the common people as well. After asserting that "the early rituals began with food and drink [with roasting of pork and grain, excavating the ground in the form of a pot, fashioning a clay handle to beat an earthen drum] as if by these means they would indicate their reverence for the ghosts and spirits 夫禮之初，始諸飲食 .... 猶若可以致敬于鬼神," the Han Confucius of the *Record* is made to elaborate:

> Therefore, with dark-colored liquor in the room and ritual vessel placed near the door, the brownish liquor would be placed in the hall and the clear kind in the courtyard below. The sacrificial victims would be displayed, while the tripods and containers stand prepared. Stringed instruments, zithers, pipes, sonorous stones, bells, and drums would be lined up, while the invocations and benedictions would be carefully worded. The aim of all this is to bring down the spirits from above, including their ancestors [one textual variant: and lift up their ancestors]. It serves also to rectify the relations

between ruler and subjects, to strengthen the feelings between fathers and sons, to induce harmony between brothers, to put in order the ranks of high and low, and to assign proper places to husbands and wives. This may be said to secure the blessing of Heaven.[35]

Theism in the Western European or classical Indian sense may have been wanting in ancient Chinese culture, but other loci of transcendence as powerful as any similar system's are readily discernible. While the enjoinment to praying individually may have received only ambiguous assessment by Confucius, no student of early Chinese culture with a passage like the one just quoted in mind can overlook the importance of ritual, centrally defined as various forms of state and communal divinations and sacrifices, that must be revered and practiced as lifelong obligations. It is in respect to ritual and the systematic elaboration given to the subject by the disciples of Confucius in antiquity that, in fact, defines the true meaning of "teaching" or *jiao*.

One such striking example of the development of Confucian teachings (as striking perhaps as, say, how the sacrament of penance or extreme unction in later Roman Catholic theology has evolved from the putative teachings of Jesus in the Gospels) is on the very word *jiao* itself. Whereas Confucius was famously described early as "the master [who] would not speak on the strange, the violent, the unruly, and the spiritual" (*Analects* 7. 21), the Han Confucian bureaucrats compiling and writing the *Record of Rites* made sure that this picture of him (so dear to contemporary loyalists as a reliable depiction of Confucius's "humanism" or "secularism") was completely *reversed* when the occasion demanded it. In the 25th chapter on "The Meaning of Sacrifices 祭義," on which the well-being of the entire sociopolitical realm depended, the Han Confucius was made to define the meaning of ghost and spirit in the following dialogue:

Zaiwuo [the disciple] said, "I hear the names of ghosts and spirits, but I don't know what they mean." The Master said, "*Qi* [pneumatic vitality?] is the fullness of spirit; the *po*-soul is the fullness of ghost. That which joins ghost and spirit is the ultimate of teachings 氣也者，神之盛也；魄也者，鬼之盛也；合鬼與神，教之至也.[36]

What the remark attributed to Confucius here renders irrefutably apparent is the fact that *jiao* as understood by Han ritual theorists already takes on religious coloration and connotation. This does not mean, however, that such religiosity can be reduced to "beliefs," an abiding temptation for much of the Western understanding of religion. Hardly something inherently propositional or creedal, what the Confucian *jiao* points to is rather a set of activities, a form of ritual intended for efficacious communion and intercourse between the human and non-human realms. As such, the remark still may sound in modern ears rather "naturalistic," but even if we regard the words spirit (*shen*) and soul (*po*), for that very reason, as some psycho-phyiscal elements associated with the human person, the definition itself is no less "religious" than when later Daoists claim that demons and gods are resident deities of our visceral systems. It is only in this light, in fact, that we can understand more fully both the vehemence and the propriety of the assertion by the well-known Tang poet-official Han Yu: "In antiquity those who taught (*jiao zhe*) took only one [position]. Now those who teach would take three [positions]."[37] Han's meaning should be quite clear, for his words signal his anguish over the contest of Confucianism by the arrival of both Daoism and Buddhism. However, his point throughout his essay "On the Origin of Dao," as shown by his painful equivocations over the titular word he unfortunately also had to share with rival religions, is not about how his own cherished tradition of Confucian belief and practices might be a different beast from the other two *jiao*.

As in so much polemical rhetoric both within and between religious traditions, the conflict, rather, centers on what one regards as truth and falsehood, norm and deviancy, in sum, orthodoxy and heterodoxy.

If *jiao* as a Chinese word by early medieval time already embraced a zone of meaning that seems to encompass a similar area for the word "religion" in modern English and European languages (at least in French, German, Italian, Spanish, and Portugese, to my knowledge), what then may be the definition of this word, one may justly ask at the close of this section of our discussion, in the context of its Western usage? The answer to this question can fill volumes, for the question, in fact, has persistently haunted the academic study of religion in the West since the Enlightenment. If one runs through a few most familiar names in the canonical history of Western scholarship on religion such as Jean Bodin (sixteenth century), David Hume (eighteenth century) Karl Marx, Fredrich Engels, E. B. Tyler, F. Max Müller, James Frazer (nineteenth century), William James, Claude Lévy-Bruhl, Bronislaw Malinowski, Emile Durkheim, Sigmund Freud, Rudolf Otto, and Mircea Eliade (twentieth century), one can encounter as many definitions of what religion is as there are scholars themselves. But what is noteworthy, firstly, is that *none* of these savants would dream of identifying Christianity as the sole, defining subject of his investigation. More often than not, their overriding aim is to develop an understanding of religion that would far exceed the phenomenological scope of a particular religion. Secondly, we should remember that the term translated as "religion" was a rare word in the New Testament, used only twice in Acts 26: 5 and James 1: 26–27, but the Greek *thrêskeia* here meaning worship, cult, rite, and religious service—hardly a peculiar invention or possession of Christian theism alone—was employed throughout the ancient Mediterranean world to designate a variety of activities.[38] Like the Han Yu of China cited above, the author of the *Epistle of James* is interested in distinguishing polemically between true and false religion, between "pure and unsullied religion" (*thrêskei kathara kai amiantos*) and its worldly contrast. Indeed, religious traditions seldom refer to themselves as a religion; for the Christians, the self-referential metaphor may be "the faith" (for example, Acts 6: 7; Ephesians 4: 13) or "the gospel" (good news); for Judaism, the *Torah* (the Law); for Islam, *din* (the law) or *sunna* (the path, the practice); and for Buddhism, the *Dharma* (the Law).

Etymologically, moreover, the word religion has a Latin root, but the stems may be multiple. One view would consider the term as coming from *religare*, the verb to tie or to bind together, a physical action that in much discursive usage would refer first to physical objects (like mooring a boat) but metaphorically may anticipate either the kind of Durkheimian thesis on religion as a form of social cohesiveness or the sort of constraint and discipline imposed by a religious tradition.[39] A second theory, however, traces the root to a different Latin word, and for our purpose here, I can do no better than to quote at length a Chicago colleague's provocative interpretation:

> In his dialogue, *De natura deorum*, written about 45 B.C., Cicero [2. 72] placed in the mouth of the Stoic Balbo an etymology of the adjective *religious* as being derived from *relegere* meaning to gather together, to collect, to go over again, to review mentally, to repeat. Balbo proposes that, "those who carefully reviewed and went over again all that pertained to the rituals of the gods were called religious from *relegere*." His argument requires that this exegetical activity be understood as a constant preoccupation. Although the etymology is most likely false, it remains a shrewed insight, based on observation, of a significant (perhaps, even distinctive) characteristic of religious thought.

Almost 2000 years later, in 1907, working from a similar grounding in observation but from radically different presuppositions, Freud, in his brief essay "Obsessive Acts and Religious Practices," proposed an analogy between "what are called obsessive acts in neurotics and those of religious observances by means of which the faithful give expression to their piety." While there is much in Freud's subsequent genetic account that is problematic, his original description of the obsessiveness common to both neurosis and religion as:

> *little* preoccupations, performances, restrictions and arrangements in certain activities of everyday life . . . elaborated by *petty modifications* . . . [and] *little* details
> . . . [the] tendency to displacement . . . [which] turns apparently *trivial* matters into those of great and urgent importance

remains, . . . , the most telling description of a significant (perhaps, even distinctive) characteristic activity that I know.[40]

Whether one agrees with the first explanation (that religion signifies some form of social and cultural forces effective for binding together a community or society) or with the second one (that religion represents "the rethinking of each little detail in a text (Cicero), [and] the obsession with the significance and perfection of each little action (Freud)",) it should be apparent that these exegetical considerations are noteworthy. They point to a practice or a mode of behavior the fundamental significance of which is functional—not doctrinal or substantive—for the group no less than for the individual. Understood in this manner, the word *religion* with its etymological overtones may provide, indeed, *a generic term* that would more readily enable resonant linkage with *jiao* or *zongjiao* in the Chinese context of pervasive ritualism than the peculiar worship of a triune deity premised on a highly particularized set of doctrines.[41]

3

State and Religion in Antiquity

ENDING THIS DETOUR built on another aspect of "the term question" often deemed "interminable" in the study of Chinese religions returns us to the subject at hand to see what a part of recent scholarship has to say about state and religion in China's antiquity. Two salient features seem to have emerged as part of the consensus.

The first concerns the origin of religion, and escalating archeological evidence reveals that forms of religious beliefs and practices are evident already in the earliest stratum of Chinese cultural life. The second is that, for long stretches of Chinese history and its dominant cultural strains, religion or traffic with "the sacred" is nothing if not in many of its crucial aspects family bound in Chinese civilization. The family, both as household and as clan, remains the one social unit that defines the ideals and behavior supposedly applicable to all levels of society, from the highest echelon of royalty to the lowliest peasant. Kin relations and hierarchy along with the exercise of authority within the family provide a literal homolog to the structures and norms of civic governance.[1] Surveying the long periods of imperial—and, even pre-imperial—history, one may risk a generalization by claiming that the royal (and later, the imperial) metaphor is firmly based and erected upon the familial metaphor. The familial metaphor, however, also mediates and manifests the Chinese relation to the sacred, a form of "familism" that historian of religion Joseph Kitagawa used to refer to the peculiar character of Chinese religious culture.[2] This is why Needham's "halls and palaces" no less than distinctive ancestral shrines (zongmiao) can assume a significance and importance that rival, and at times threaten to supplant, the particular edifices set aside for specifiable religious functions, the separately consecrated temples and abbeys of other traditions.

Evidence for the high antiquity of Chinese religious life, according to recent archeological scholarship, may go back to an astonishing date of 16,000 B.C.E. and reaching down to the fourth and third millenia B.C.E. The geographical reach of the various early regional farming cultures spans huge portions of northern, northwestern, and southern China, including the river valleys of the Yangzi River. Material remains unearthed at Zhoukoudian, near Beijing, in the eastern part of Inner Mongolia (at Xinglongwa near Aohanqi), and at the Fangshan and Yaoshan sites (near modern Hangzhou of Zhejiang Province) during the Liangzhu period (*ca.* 3500–2500 B.C.E.) already suggest a certain preoccupation and emphasis that can readily be regarded as consonant with religious ideology of much later history. Edifices, inclusive of peculiar mounds, altar-like elevations, and grave sites, and artifacts such as tomb objects, ceramic pottery, jewelry, and human as well as animalistic figures all indicate a persistent and immense concern for the dead and their treatment.[3]

Such a concern, of course, is hardly the exclusive property of ancient Chinese religiosity, and different cultures have recorded and displayed a variety of customs and attitudes toward the dead. In spite or because of the widespread fear of pollution caused by the corpse, the Greeks, for example, were known for their fastidious death rituals[4] and burial customs, the latter of which included, in remarkable semblance to the Chinese, elaborate gifts for the dead as material possessions befitting their stations in their lives, regularized sacrifices, and the perpetual caring of grave sites by descendants.[5] Heroes of a particular locality, apotheosized while still living (for example, Oedipus, Philoctetes in dramatic enactment) or heroicized after death, would receive post-mortem honor and memorialization in the cultic activities of competitive games or *agones*.[6] If the feature emerging at the early stage of Chinese cultural development seems to betoken a belief "in the continuation of life after death: a person had to be equippped in death with those items that had been essential in life,"[7] what makes this belief distinctive is not the mere affirmation of a post-mortem existence or even how the care for the welfare of the dead must parallel living conditions (for example, tomb pottery filled with grain). Rather, the anxiety driven by the dread that the entombed deceased differentiated as particular classes of the dead could still command overwhelming power to bestow good or evil on the living is what distinguishes Shang religion. Later attitudes and practices, enhanced by Confucian doctrines, would "rationalize" such fears and render them as the just reverence and concern for these classes of the dead, namely, the ancestors. The elaborate ordering of ancestral relations to the living so as to preserve the status of kinship (biological and artificial, as we shall see presently) would mark the bedrock character of one enduring and dominant form of Chinese religiosity, a form that unites in itself the socially discordant elements of familial, communal, and political life.

That kingship existed relatively early in Chinese political history is known to all students of that civilization. That ancestor worship appeared in the period of the Shang (ca. 1570–1045 B.C.E.) and became, from its very origin, a practice firmly tied to rulership has also found ample documentation and exploration in contemporary scholarship. Material evidence from the period of King Wu Ding (?–1189 B.C.E.) suggests progressive increment of royal claim to knowledge and power through certain ritual activities associated with the worship. At the cult center located at Xiaotun, according to the Western scholar who is one of the leading authorities in the world on the subject, "here were the burials of royal ancestors, whose powerful assistance the living king and his dependents solicited with cult and whose spirits offered pyromantic guidance about the conduct of the dynasty's affairs."[8]

Recognizing the importance of ancestors as objects of worship in Shang religion does not mean that they were the sole objects. Students of religion accustomed to the taxonomical distinction between monotheism and polytheism may find it difficult to sort out the blurred sense of hierarchy and division of power among the several revered loci of transcendence, such as certain natural phenomena like rivers, mountains, and the sun; groups of deceased "spirits" (further divided—at least by current scholarship—into Former Lords, predynastic ancestors, and dynastic ancestors) and the solitary High God or *di*. The last figure, still eliciting scholarly debate as to whether it refers to a separate Higher Power or a Supreme ancestor,[9] was forever assimilated into imperial ideology when, in the waning days of the Warring States period, two rulers of the states of Qin and Qi simultaneously assumed in 288 B.C.E. this divine title as eastern and western *di*. Thereafter, the victorious Qin and all subsequent emperors through the Qing dynasty clung to this name. Much later still, in the late Ming and the Qing periods, the nomenclature finds adoption, first by Catholic and then by Protestant missionaries, for the translation of God in Christian scriptures and theology.[10] That it is fast becoming an accepted convention among contemporary Western scholars to translate *di* as "thearch" further accentuates the religious overtones of the term, and the imperial institution's deliberate appropriation for its own perpetual use bespeaks astute awareness, not ignorance, of the name's immense significance.[11]

The "Former Lords (*xiangong* 先公)," another group of powers, are also not of "royal origin," but their participation in the Shang cult system indicates their significance therein in the overall authority of the selected dead that impinges on the most important affairs of the living. The communal concerns relative to weather, crops, natural vicissitudes (earthquakes, fires, floods, eclipses), and warfare would require the king's obligatory attention, but so would such concerns of his person as health, illness, child-bearing and the fertility of his consorts, and the rectitude of ritual enactment.[12] Despite the costly and intricate system of oracle bone inscription designed to determine the probity of sacrifices (through divination) offered to ancestors, to solicit their assistance, and to prevent their maledictions indicates the elevated status of ancestors, the fact that the king was recorded to be both the central practitioner and often the unerring prognosticator of unfolding events (as in the case of Wu Ding) further reveals "divination's validating role."[13] The nature of the religious activity, in sum, firmly establishes an intimate and reciprocal relationship between royalty and, through that institution, state power and authority and the realm of sacral kinship.

What we should remember most about this facet of Shang's religion, however, is that it does not merely advocate the worship of ancestors stemming from natural genealogy. It does not reflect simply an activity, as later Confucians would interpret it, arising out of the "natural" desire of humans to "love one's parents" (qinqin), such that, as Matteo Ricci would have it still later, it is an exercise of secular virtue that in itself poses little conflict with the claims and norms of his "true religion."[14] In Ricci's ingenious re-interpretation as part of his Christian apologetics, increasingly accepted by later Chinese intellectuals who themselves might not even be sympathetic with Catholicism, rituals performed for ancestors were merely acts of reverence and commemoration of one's immediate, and by gradation, one's more removed forebearers. This line of argument, as is well-known, led eventually to the Rites Controversy and the official repudiation of Ricci's teaching on the matter of ancestor worship by the Vatican. On the other hand, what the contemporary scholarship of someone like David Keightley has irrefutably established is rather that the "ancestors" venerated by the Shang royal house are powers not only generated by blood ties but are deliberately created as a form of religious culture.

The most distinctive feature characterizing the maintenance of this ancestral system is thus its institutionalization of the ritual of ancestor-making that, paradoxically, depersonalizes actual kin relations. Periodic rituals not only sacrifice to real forebearers of the royal house but also "canonize," like the Roman Church does its saints, other unrelated "ancestors" for the divine pantheon.[15]

Beyond that somewhat far-fetched comparison with Western Christianity, Hindu rituals based on later Dharmaśāastras, Purāṇas, and medieval expansion of Vedic doctrines that helped to proliferate and conventionalize actions concerned with the disposal of the corpse (cremation for the standard adult, earth burial and gathering of bone fragments for eventual deposition in a sacred river for the dead among children, certain ascetics, the suicidal, and others of untimely deaths) and the "making" of the ancestor (pitṛ, literally father or mother, parent) from the disembodied spirit or ghost (preta) provide even more interesting elements of comparison with the ancient Chinese practice. Crucial to the rationale of the Indian system is the successful creation of the ancestor after cremation of the actual body through construction of a temporary "body" by means of regularized ritual enactments (e.g., formation of a cooked rice ball ten days after cremation, spreading different food grains on the burial ground, and the donning of different garment or materials by the chief mourner). The climactic event of the sapiṇḍīkaraṇa ritual, wherein different rice balls representing different generations are blended, is designed to unite

the newly created ancestor with those of preceding generations.[16]

It should be remembered, of course, that the Hindic
burial rites and rituals devoted to nurturing the ancestors
(the meticulous performance of which in pre-modern times
could be as regular as monthly observances) are for the
ultimate purpose of ensuring eventual promotion for the
ancestors from their otherworldly abode to a better path of
rebirth. Until Indian culture entered China with Buddhism,
the religious custom of this nature in Chinese antiquity bore
a different meaning and purpose than that of transmigration, or, as in certain teachings of later religious Daoism, the
expiation of ancestral guilt and the elevation of the deceased into the realms of gods and immortals. The worship
of both kin forebears (males and females) and of unrelated
powers designated ritually as ancestors (*zu*), including such
powers as the Former Lords, in China's high antiquity first
and foremost served the interest of the state and its sovereign, and in this capacity it thus

> laid the seeds of a practice maintained throughout China's
> imperial history. The canonization of dead officers, who, like
> the royal ancestors, were capable of cursing the living and of
> receiving sacrifices, demonstrated that high status in this life,
> conferred by the king, could be maintained, with the help of
> the king's descendants, in the next. View of the afterlife thus
> served to validate status relations among the living.[17]

It should be apparent that such a ritual ideology, which
purports to establish, sustain, and perpetuate the authority
and power of a royal house, can have no better name than
a state religion, because the daily, mundane welfare of all
subjects of a particular domain, in theory, are affected by
it. The ritual and belief associated with this religion, in fact,
did not change with the arrival of the Zhou periods (western
and eastern) that followed the Shang. If nothing else, ritual

bronzes indicate that "the ancestors were, it would appear, an all-embracing force, and all action was taken with them in mind," since material contents of tombs and inscriptions "reveal a concern with ancestors, status, relationships with others, and the legitimating force of the past."[18] This concern over time, in fact, would gain in intensity and importance when new material resources became available during the Zhou, as when costly bronze bells were used for ancestral sacrifice and burial objects, while banquets for ancestors utilized an abundance and variety of ritual vessels elaborately cast.[19] Even at the time of the Warring States, when the expanded ideal of conquest made territorial cults threaten the supremacy of the ancestral cult in religious performance,[20] the latter's significance and importance were patently revived and upheld—proleptically—in a Han document like the *Record of Rites*. Moreover, the history of art and archeology would seem to indicate that the process of "diffusion" had set in during the Eastern Zhou and had continued all the way to the Han, when a royal cultic activity was progressively made more widespread to lower echelon nobles and to perhaps even the commoners. The development could be seen in "the increasing attention paid to funerary rites . . . and the compilations of detailed codes for mortuary rites"[21] prescribed not only for royalty but also for the literate elites and, through them, to the people at large. This process of extending the claims and focus of ritual from lineage temple to the family graveyard undoubtedly played a crucial role in expanding an ancient form of religiosity into an enduring and pervasive norm for vitually all Chinese posterity.[22] At the same time in the later Han, as we shall see at the end of this section of the study, the practice of "canonizing (*feng* 封)"—by means of bureaucratic appeal to the imperial court—worthy individuals after death whose significance was not based on kinship but on both narrated merit and constructed lineage, found its climactic expression in elevating Confucius into a figure of perpetual, obligatory worship for both emperors and subjects. Daniel Overmyer is unerring when he observes that "the attitude of the traditional Chinese state toward the religious activities of the people was an expression of its own religious commitments. From its beginnings in the Shang dynasty . . . , much of the authority of the state was understood to be derived from the ancestors and deities worshipped by the ruler and his officials."[23]

There are three reasons why this study has dwelt at length on such a venerable topic as ancestor worship. Despite its familiarity, I want to emphasize the implications of such worship for understanding the character of Chinese state power and authority. First, I want to attempt to clear up the misconception, proposed by both past and even modern interpretations, that this form of worship merely betokens acts of reverence for kindred dead. As we have seen, Shang religious culture provides us with the important discovery that ancestor-making was much more than a ceremonious act dictated by the obligations of kinship. It was, rather, a ritual designed to recruit and invoke agencies of transcendence, wherein ancestors were to be transformed from a term of kinship to become symbols of divine power. Confucius's words that "sacrificing to spirits not of one's own is obsequious" (*Analects* 2. 24),[24] in this light, provide a verdict of poignant irony, because they might, unintentionally, confirm the findings of contemporary scholarship. Although his remark might have been meant to target once more the vaunting transgressions of feudal nobles who would arrogate to themselves royal prerogatives and practices, it might also reveal Confucius's ignorance that part of Shang royal ritual was precisely such an "obsequious" act of making and worshipping other ancestral spirits.

Second, correlatively speaking, the cultic functions of such worship for the maintenance and flourishing of state power belies the conviction, common even among Chinese savants, that the foundational ideals of the Chinese state from antiquity are essentially secular. Not only is the word "theocracy" increasingly used by contemporary scholars to describe Shang government, but the powers ascribed to the ancestors in inscriptional records contradict also the protracted claim, as noted earlier, that the Chinese lacked a sense of religion because the people supposedly had no clear conception of a deity like the Western God. As we have seen, the ancient Shang and Zhou people might not have developed a monotheistic system of values and beliefs, but the combined pantheon of natural and ancestral forces (the latter in discourse also thought to be part of nature) offers a wide-ranging representation of sacral potency. If this somewhat hodgepodge pantheon, as enumerated in the *Zhouli*, for example, could nonetheless claim to affect virtually all the vital affairs of state and its subjects—war, harvest, weather, plagues, flood, divinations, astrological observations, and the personal well-being of the head of state[25]—then is there any theoretical justification for insisting on the need of a personal deity for defining religiosity, for the Chinese or anyone else?

The question posed above to which a resolute "No" must be the intended answer also provides a parenthetical opportunity to clarify my use of the word "transcendence" in this study that had been queried by my kind and official discussant during the occasion of the Master Hsüan Hua Lecture. The clarification is simple: my use follows the uncomplicated definition of a recent standard reference in defining the term as "divine attribute, existing above and independently of the material world."[26] So understood, the term's usage in the present context of historical Chinese cultures ought not to be differently construed than when the word is employed for beings and powers alleged to be possessive of such attributes in Greek, Indian, and African cultures, to name only those I have referred to for *comparative* purpose. Above all, the term—once more, another part of the "interminable term question" endemic to scholarship on China (!)—does not intend to invoke the peculiar meaning invested therein by European modernism in the philosophy of religion, exemplified by Rudolf Otto (1869–1937). His book of 1924, *Das Heilige: über das irrationale in der Idee des Göttlichichen und sein Verhältnis zum Rationalen*, and its 1929 sequel in two volumes, *Aufsätze das Numinose betreffend* had exerted considerable impact on both sides of the Atlantic with his depiction of "the Holy" as a form of transcendence that is "wholly other (*Das ganz Andere*)," the sub-title, in fact, of the first volume of his *Aufsätze*.[27] This form of "the Holy" in Otto's understanding defines the religious essentially as a kind of monstrous numen that at once fascinates and terrifies, attracts and repels. The paradoxical attribute thus points to both the conception of the Romantic notion of sublimity and its more ancient source, the *Peri hypsos* (On the Sublime) attributed to the Greek rhetorician and theorist Longinus. That Otto's ideas ultimately also echo the descriptions of the deity in Judaic-Christian theism is plain,[28] but whether those descriptions should be regarded as normative for all ideas about "transcendence" as wholly discontinuous otherness is once more a dispute of "the term question." In the end, my use of such a term no less than my approach to the study of Chinese religion(s) is premised on the possibility of discursive continuity along with respect for distinctiveness and peculiarity. These are the terms of the comparison that I have chosen to follow in much of my writings on religion and on literature. As Jonathan Z. Smith repeatedly points out, however,

> there is nothing 'natural' about the enterprise of comparison. Similarity and difference are not 'given'. They are the result of mental operations. . . . A comparison is a disciplined exag-

geration in the service of knowledge. It lifts out and strongly marks certain features within difference as being of possible intellectual significance, expressed in the rhetoric of their being 'like' in some stipulated fashion. Comparison provides the means by which *we* 're-vision' phenomena as *our* data in order to solve *our* theoretical problems.[29]

Insistence on absolute cultural disparity and uniquess, as a cultural critic concerned with Chinese studies trenchantly reminds us recently, runs the risk of perpetuating and objectifying dubious dichotomies of all kinds.[30]

The third and final implication of ancestor worship is the enduring influence and importance of the familial metaphor in state ritual no less than in the diffused Confucian discourse on politics and ethics that seeks to shape and uphold a particular ideal for the nature and authority of the state. The ideals of ancestor worship on the level of the state, as Howard J. Wechsler wisely observes, "help to shape political alignments, territorial divisions, and the organization of authority."[31] To be sure, the practice of ancestor worship in the commoner's household might have declined with modernity (though the activity certainly continues even today in pockets of the Chinese diaspora worldwide), but the significance of the ancestral shrine (*zongmiao, taimiao* 宗廟, 太廟) for imperial governance remained constant from pre-Qin times to the Qing. For good reason, the cultic activities associated with this site and symbol have long been a subject of intense scrutiny by ritualists.

The sustained debate descending from the time of the Han throughout imperial history had developed along two lines of controversial inquiry. The first concerned the structure and number of the royal ancestral temple itself: internal arrangement, numbers of ancestors to which temples are to be erected, the criteria for maintaining certain ancestral "spirit tablets (*shenzhu pai* 神主牌)" in perpetuity and for removing others, and the criteria for designating certain ancestors as the Great Ancestor (*taizu* 太祖) or First Ancestor (*shizu* 始祖).[32] The second topic of repeated debate was whether the sacrifice to Heaven (*ji* 祭 or *si tian* 祀天)— the sole prerogative of the emperor as Son of Heaven—or the sacrifice to ancestors— a ritual practicable to both ruler and subjects—should be accorded supreme eminence is also a familiar theme in the history of Chinese ritualism.[33] The controversy between these two rituals notwithstanding, their unresolved tension actually points up once more the ambitious and aggressive tendency of imperial apologists to make certain that their sovereign—and the state as an extension of such sovereignty—would succeed in making the most inclusive claim of absolute power. What delimits that power are the two overlapping spheres of its exercise affirmed for the imperial monarch: the cosmic realm of nature as epitomized by Heaven and Earth and the realm of the humans as defined by the ethical and political principles of their relations (*lun* 倫). As stated succinctly in the *Records of Rites*: "all things originate from Heaven [and] humans originate from the ancestor. This is why one offers food and drink to the Exalted *di*. 萬物本乎天, 人本乎祖, 此所以配上帝也."[34]

Despite noticeable discrepancies internal to the received text (for example, inconsistent or contradictory numbers recorded for royal ancestral temples), that classic discourse on ritual makes apparent, nonetheless, that just as the supreme ruler (by his assumption of the name, Son of Heaven or *tian zi*) is held accountable to Heaven and Earth in the governance of his people, his responsibility to his forbears is no less serious and heavy. For good reason, therefore, Wechsler has concluded that "judging from archaeological, epigraphical, and literary evidence, there was little or no differentiation in ancient times between such structures as the royal residence, the hall of government, the ancestral temple, or even such 'cosmic' edifices as the Hall of Light (*Ming-t'ang*). The palace was a temple and vice versa."[35]

One example of how the mutually reinforcing concerns of revering both the forces of nature and the obligations of kinship would actually be translated into the policies of governance that could be justly termed a form of state or political religion (*zhengzhi zongjiao* 政治宗教),[36] we may turn to the Han compendium again. In the chapter on "Royal Regulations" (*Wangzhi* 王制), it is prescribed that prior to an inspectional expedition by the ruler (the Son of Heaven), he must sacrifice to the Exalted *Di* and offer the Yi Sacrifice at the Altar of the Earth and the Zhao Sacrifice at the Ancestral Temple (5. 23). For a punitive expedition, there is the added specific prescription that he must "receive the mandate from his ancestors." After the expedition, he must return to report to his ancestors on the captivity of those culpable and use the left ears cut off from his enemies for the rite honoring his ancestors (5. 27). During the grand tour of inspecting his fiefdom expected of the ruler every five years, this is what he is supposed to do:

> In the year's second month, the Son of Heaven would visit the East and honor Mount Tai. By burning wood he would sacrifice to Heaven and to the mountains and rivers. Granting audience to the feudal princes, he would seek out the hundred-year-olds and visit them; order the Grand Music-Master to present poems of different states so as to observe the manners of the people; order the supervisers of markets to bring forth lists of prices so as to observe what the people like and dislike, and whether they set their minds on excess and love the perverse; order the superintendent of rites to investigate the seasons and months, and fix the days and render uniform the tuning bells, the ceremonies, the musical [instruments], all measurements, and the fashions of garments.
>
> If there were spirits of mountains and rivers unattended to, it would be considered an act of irreverence, and for such

an irreverent [lord] the ruler would cut off part of his territory. Where rites of the ancestral temple (*zongmiao*) are improper, this would be considered an unfilial act. The rank of the unfilial one would be reduced. Those who would change the rites and alter music are the disobedient ones, and such disobedient ones the ruler would banish. Those who would modify statutory measures and sartorial fashions are rebellious, and the ruler would punish the rebellious ones by force (5. 22)

Whether a passage like this represents an accurate report of royal practice of the Zhou or an anachronistic projection of Confucian idealists for the newly established imperial regime of the Han is not my concern here. Rather, I have taken pains to quote this entire passage because it is a comprehensive articulation of what arguably remains a set of cherished ideals for the benevolent or virtuous state in the Chinese consciousness. Some of these ideals certainly continue down to the present. Within this ethos fostered by religious devotion to Heaven and to the ancestors, the cherished ideals are those promoting uniformity, orderliness, continuity, conformity, and compliance with group norms and even group tastes, in sharp contrast to the predilection for difference in individuality, originality, creativity, and self-initiative championed by other civilizations. Ancestral temples may no longer dot the landscape of any contemporary Chinese community, but the regard for kin relations, it need hardly be said, can be as tenacious as ever. For good reason, therefore, contemporary Chinese scholars not fully persuaded by the Western advocacy of human rights can argue for the care of the elders, a logical outgrowth of the doctrine of filial piety, as a part of the rights of elders that modern Asian states like China and Taiwan duly seek to uphold by legislation.[37]

The weight of the ancestors in Chinese socio-political life, however, does not reside merely in the derived obligation, moral and legal, of the young to care for their elderly kin. As we have seen in the passage cited above, ancestors of imperial ideology constitute the authorizing agency for exercising one of the most important facets of royal power: that of waging war. Through proper ritual the ancestors would grant to the Son of Heaven the mandate to fight, and he, upon his campaign's completion, must report back to them for the disposition of the prisoners. The ancestors's demand for the prisoners's severed left ears, in this regard, is no less exacting than Saul's request from David for one hundred foreskins of the Philistines, the enemies of the Israelite king (1 Sam. 18: 17–27). Conversely, in the same line of reasoning, permitting a defeated state, as when the invincibly powerful Qin had conquered the Eastern Zhou (*ca.* bet. 250 and 221 B.C.E.), to continue its sacrifices to ancestors betokens an act of generosity and peace-making (*Shiji* 5). Given the important role that ancestors play in the religious foundation of the ancient dynasties, it is no wonder that the subsequent dominant discourse on politics and ethics developed by the Confucians would emphasize persistently the near complete correspondence between family or clan and the state, the two social domains that would mirror each other in beliefs and values, in practice and activities.[38]

One imporant implication of this correspondence between family and state is the accepted and entrenched ascription of the parental metaphor to the ruler. Beginning with such ancient sources as the *Classic of Documents* and the *Classic of Poetry* and continuing with echoes in such Warring States thinkers like Mengzi and Xunzi, rulers are repeatedly described as parents (*fumu* 父母). To be sure, the Confucian disciples associate this metaphor with the care of the people. However, first with the Qin ruler's assumption of *di* as a self-designation, and subsequently with later emperors assuming in rapid succession the titles of *zu* and *zong* (both words mean "ancestor"), the imperial arrogation of kinship nomenclatures clearly indicates a policy of fostering status and control. Not only does the emperor mediate the blessings and cursings incurred from his worship of imperial ancestors, but through the titular claim his person has also become since Qin Shihuangdi the designated "ancestor" of his subjects. The people are, in principle, completely beholden to the godlike authority of a supreme patriarch who now bears the oxymoronic name of "living ancestor"—beholden, because the ancestor (*zu*) metaphor, as stated in the *Record of Rites*, has transformed the political sovereign into an undisputed creator or origin of human life. As a celebrated modern Marxist historian, Fan Wenlan, had remarked about Zhou civilization,

> regardless of whether it was the ruling class or that of the ruled, the worship of ancestors occupied the sole position of importance in their ideology. Filial piety was publicly affirmed to be the highest moral virtue, to such an extent that no venerated deity or doctrine of another religion could serve as a substitute for ancestor worship and the way of filiality. Historically, this is the distinguishing character of the Han race. Religion could not take deep root amidst the Han race because the clan rules functioned as a form of resistance 宗教在漢民族不能生深根，宗法是起了抵抗作用的.[39]

Although Fan fails to recognize that ancestor worship so valorized by clan rules was already the religion *par excellence* that had taken the deepest root in Han society, underpinning the structures and principles of both pre-imperial and imperial government, his words still deserve our sober consideration.

This development effectively justifies what I have described elsewhere as the homolog of virtues created by the Confucian discourse and extolled by that discourse as a practice proper to both the political and familial domains.[40] Filial piety (*xiao* 孝) is singled out as the unifying virtue that can mutate readily from familial reverence for the father into loyalty (*zhong* 忠) for the ruler (*Classic of Filial Piety* 5), and thus the filial person, by definition, would not be disposed to affront his superiors or incite a rebellion (*Analects* 1.2). According to this principle, therefore, the filial subject as citizen would not—and should not—engage in any act of public dissent, let alone the sort of subversive, recalcitrant activities as ritual negligence, altering customs and rites, and modifying standard measures and fashions as listed in the cited passage from the *Record of Rites* quoted above. Rather, the citizen, as filial child and political subject, would not merely accept the de facto control of the sovereign in the public realm and the *pater familias* in the home, but would also embrace the principle that there is really no such thing as a zone or region of the personal—of private desire, knowledge, action, and possession—that ought to lie beyond the reach and concern of the totalitarian patriarch and his governance—at court or at home.[41] For good reason, therefore, filial piety by the Han dynasty had already found institutionalization as a criterion for selecting worthy officials, because it "became a core value in the Chinese web of interpersonal relationships, an axis linking the individual human being, his family, and his society."[42] The linking axis of this setting is loyalty to domestic and social community that, in modern rhetoric, easily elides into patriotism (*aiguo* 愛國).

The Han practice of rewarding filial persons with official appointments not only validates the verdict of Confucius, when he cited the *Classic of Documents* in *Analects* 2.21 to say: "Simply by being a good son and friendly to his brothers a man can exert an influence upon government."[43] It brings into focus the ancient conviction of longstanding (for example Keightley's cited remark on p. 32 above) that the way the Chinese state should honor persons of paramount virtue—by definition already those who had thus served the body politic with the greatest merit—would be to make them the recipients of state-sponsored sacrifices. In the *Guoyu* 國語 or *Speeches for the States*, an anthology of alleged "sayings of rulers and prominent persons . . . drawn up for the various states of the Spring and Autumn period and subsequently supplemented from other sources,"[44] the famous Lu minister (*dafu*) Zhan Qin 展禽 (a.k.a. Liu-xia-hui 柳下惠) was recorded to have said:

> Sacrifices (*si* 祀) are the great principles (*da jie* 大節), and principles are that by which governance is accomplished. Therefore, caution must be exercised in instituting sacrifices to become the canons of the state (*guodian* 國典). . . . Here is how the sage kings instituted the sacrifices: those who provided models (*fa* 法) for the people [to emulate] would receive sacrifices; those who served diligently even unto death would receive sacrifices; those whose labor had secured the state would receive sacrifices; those who could prevail against great calamities would receive sacrifices; those who could overcome great disasters would receive sacrifices; but those who did not belong to the same clan would not be inscribed in the sacrificial canons . . . .[Such sacrifices] were extended to include the gods of mountains and rivers and of grain, for all these had meritoriously benefited the people. They reached the former worthies of noted virtue, by which [the sacrifices] became the illustrious testimony thereof. They reached the Three Luminaries [sun, moon, and stars] of heaven, for these were what the people revered. They reached the Five Phases of earth, for it was by these that reproduction and growth came about.[45]

Given the fact that by the time of the Han, part of the supreme ruler's prerogative to authorize investiture of selected "natural" powers and the worthy human dead as *legitimate* objects of state worship had already become a venerable tradition, it should be no surprise that one of the greatest cultural icons of antiquity should be recognized and thus honored. What is surprising is how little attention the topic of the post-mortem elevation of Confucius and the sustained, evolving process of turning his shrine into a temple of official state rites, have received in the study of Chinese religions until quite recently.[46]

When Confucius died in the fourth month of 479 B.C.E., according to the *Zuo Commentary* (Duke Ai 16), the Duke of Lu honored him with a personal elegy, calling him "Father Ni,"[47] the posthumous title utilizing part of the latter's honorific style of Zhongni. But there was no write-up about his household, family shrine, or activities of either descendants or disciples until the longer account by Sima Qian (*Shiji* 47) several hundred years later. That the time of the Han saw the political and social promotion of Confucian teachings and the man's status may be seen thus not merely in the luxriant description by the Grand Scribe, but also by the concrete homage allegedly paid to the deceased sage in an escalating succession of emperors, abetted by advocative lobbying of descendants and partisan officials. Despite his known contempt for Ruist scholars, the founding emperor of the Han, Liu Bang, felt obliged to make sacrifice in the Confucian shrine when passing through the State of Lu in 195 B.C.E. (*Shiji* 97). By the year 8 B.C.E., however, the minister Mei Fu 梅福 believed that "to acknowledge appropriately the Three Unities [of Xia, Shang, and Zhou as a continuous and legitimate dynastic tradition], the descendants of Confucius should be officially declared to have belonged to the lineage of Yin [Shang]." He, therefore, petitioned the Emperor Chengdi to make by decree Confucius a lineal descendant of Shang so that perpetual state-sponsored sacrifices could be established, and the final part of his argument went as follows:

> Up till now the temple of Zhongni has not left its native location of Queli, and the descendants of Mr. Kong are no better than commoners. For a sage to receive sacrifices like those of a commoner is not the will of August Heaven. If Your

Majesty could canonize (封) his sons and grandsons on the basis of Zhongni's unofficial merit (素功), then our nation (國家) would most certainly receive his blessings (必獲其福), and Your Majesty's name would endure forever like Heaven's. Why is this so? To trace out the unofficial merit of a sage in order to canonize his descendants has had no [previous] example. Sages in posterity will surely regard this as the norm (則). How could you not exert every effort to gain such an indestructible reputation![48]

Mei Fu's line of reasoning, as we can see readily, presents a refinement of the assertion by Zhan Qin cited above, but it places an even greater emphasis on the rewards to be reaped by both state and emperor as occasioned by the existential concerns of Mei's petition. The most important reason for this act of canonization, we should also notice, lies not only in the recognition of a particular person's contribution to state and society, in accordance with sacrificial statutes based on Zhan Qin's principles. That the lineage of the deceased Confucius had to be changed to make him a legitimate recipient of imperial sacrifices was, in fact, bound up with the norms of antique state religion. The justification for this move again lay first in the emperor's declaration of merit for someone who had led a life without lofty appointment. Unlike the Duke of Zhou who, in almost six subsequent centuries, would be the arch rival of Confucius in the imperial cult until the former's permanent displacement and removal from the sacrifical system in the early Tang, Confucius enjoyed neither royal kinship nor exalted rank. Mei Fu's rhetoric hence inaugurated the poignance of the twice used phrase, "unofficial merit [literally, merit without colors]," that anticipated the designation of Confucius as "uncrowned king (suwang 素王)" by admirers of later times.[49] From the perspective of the Confucian loyalists, that the master had not been recognized in his own time with high office indicted the blindness of the Zhou king and feudal princes, but that lack of discernment would now be redeemed by this proposed act of imperial canonization. The expected benefits of such changes of status and rankings of sacrifice thus would accrue not merely to the descendants but primarily and justly to the state and the sovereign who personified it. For the act to attain its proper magnitude, the shrine of Confucius—hitherto no more than a commoner's local ancestral temple—would be expanded into a national one, made legitimate by its incorporation into the state cult genealogy and structure, and its use in state worship evetually would be diffused in countless local replications.

Mei Fu's petition, declined at first by Chengdi, was eventually adopted,[50] but as Huang Chin-hsing has observed, this was only "the first move to implement the glorification of Confucius."[51] Even such an initial implementation, however, bodes ramifications far beyond the act itself to implicate the perennial debate, intermittently intensified since the Ming of Ricci's time, on whether Confucianism is a form a religion. From the perspective of the received narratives about Confucius and the teachings attributed to him, the argument certainly can be made that the historical teacher neither declared himself a founder of a "religious" movement nor advocated teachings and actions every part of which could be construed as "religious," however defined. At most, he did not challenge the religious heritage he received or dispute his culture's pervasive ritualism, much of which, as we have seen, was unambiguously religious.

On the other hand, his canonization in the later Han changes radically the *meaning* of his person and his legacy, for the profound impact Confucius was able to exert on the Chinese people and their historical civilization thereafter would henceforth not be based solely on the merit of his virtues and doctrines as a private teacher. Not only were his teachings and the partisan exegetical expansions thereof codified as state orthodoxy, but his very person became a co-opted object of worship by the state, of the state, and for the state. If one should want to use religious terminologies familiar to Western readers, it is not far-fetched to say that the Chinese state cult in the persons of the emperor and ministers were undertaking "ecclesiastical" action in such canonization, because petitions, memorials, decrees, and edicts based on repeated and concentrated exegetical re-interpretations of canonical texts (shades of the Ciceronian action that "carefully reviewed and went over again all that pertained to the rituals of the gods" as reported by Smith) joined in subsequent eras to validate posthumously and incrementally a human's worth and ratify his elevation to transcendent status.

The temple of Confucius, now justly tagged as built by imperial decree (*chijian* 敕建)—like certain Buddhist and Daoist edifices of later times similarly—also became, in the apposite terms coincidentally appearing in both book titles by Huang Chin-hsing and Thomas Wilson, a *shengyu* 聖域, literally, sacred territory, space, or ground. The one wor-shipped in this space consecrated by the state existed as an ally of the state by ritual fiat, and, as such, was expected to assist in mediating authority and benefits to the subjects of the state, because the ultimate aim of the imperial sacrific-es, as Wilson has aptly pointed out, was so to "nourish" the cult pantheon that the cosmos would be properly ordered.[52] Whether the historical Confucius ever dreamt of having such honor or infamy conferred upon him centuries after his death is no more relevant a question than if one were to ask whether the thousands of saints in the Roman Catholic Church had wished personally to be canonized. What is im-portant for us to acknowledge is that, like Catholicism, the state canonization of this Chinese sage tacitly but irrefut-ably asserted *a twofold religious claim* that revolved, in this particular mode of Chinese expression, around the issue of lineage. First, the state advanced the claim that it possessed transcendent knowledge of the subject and his descendants in question and their apposite disposition in another realm that not even the subject himself could have knowledge of. Second, its ritual action manipulating the deceased and his descendants was deemed potent enough to alter the biological history and status of the dead to benefit the living of the present and the future. To say, therefore, that the Confucian temple established by the state cult ideology did not serve a religious purpose is tantamount to saying that the shrine of St. Francis of Assisi consists of no more than a little ceremonial hut of incidental art objects.

As both Huang and Wilson's studies have shown, the process of enhancing the importance and status of the apotheosized Confucius gains scope and momentum in the following centuries. Repeatedly during the Han already, the descendants of Confucius were promoted to higher ranks so that "implicitly, [they would] henceforth perform sacrificial duty not only for their clan , but also for the government"[53] even as the number of the physical temple sites multiplied. Moreover, Han emperors such as Mingdi in 72 and Andi in 124, while visiting the Confucian temple, began to broaden the sacrificial recipients to include the seventy-two disciples of Confucius. Eventually, the alleged favorite disciple Yan Hui 顏回 also began to receive "correlative worship and continued to be so honored . . . between the Han and T'ang."[54] Since it was in this dynasty that another crucial cultural institution of historical China, the state school and examination system, had been formally and structurally established, it was no accident that the two revered teachers of antiquity, the Duke of Zhou and Confucius, were required to be worshipped by every school attendant in 59 A.D. Such a development helped to explain why by the mid-Tang period, "there were seven hundred to one thousand Confucian temples in the areas controlled by the government,"[55] many of which were decreed to be erected on the ground of even the humblest unit of state-sponsored education. The educational and political systems throughout many periods of historical China arguably were institutions that provided mutual support, and thus "the rise of the cult of Confucius in the T'ang was to reinforce the *religious* import of rites *cum* education."[56] Thus again, it was no accident that the full emergence of the Confucian temple-school occured in the Tang.

During the few centuries after the collapse of the Han when territorial China fell into long stretches of political disunion, social division, and cultural fragmentation, the local temple at Confucius's native region of Qufu suffered repeated destruction and ruin. Moreover, the legitimate line of the sage's descendants at this time might have come to an end, but that did not stop the rulers in various parts of a divided empire from designating officially certain living members of a clan surnamed Kong 孔 in the native region to continue the legal lineage and therby rebuild and preserve both temple and worship. Throughout the period of disunity called the North-South era (420–588), the specifications for sacrificial objects (for example, the size of the animals, the required vessels of bells and chimes, costumes) and ritual patterns (how many rows of dancers, prescribed movements) were progressively modified. Similarly, the posthumous enoblement of Confucius's ranked status escalated through the dynastic changes. By 739 of the Kaiyuan period in the Tang, Confucius was bestowed the title of Wenxuan Wang 文宣王 or King of Manifest Culture. Some six centuries later, the Ming's first emperor would remove "posthumous noble titles of all the gods and spirits of the [imperial] pantheon, except for that of Confucius, who retained his title."[57]

Even so brief a survey of this process may provoke another obvious question: why was the elevation of the Sage so important to the emperor and his cultic minions? The answer is simple: for various emperors lasting nearly two millennia, the importance of Confucius receiving imperially sponsored sacrifices finds crystallization in the political and moral legitimacy that the ritual mutually conferred on both parties. Just as the state's recognition of Confucius and its continual process of canonizing his descendants were indicative of its own moral discernment and enlightenment, so the designated descendants's fulfilment of their ritual duties on behalf of the state betokened their acknowledgement of the regime's legitimacy. Small wonder that when one of the descendants declined an imperial audience with the founding emperor of the Ming (perhaps because of the fact that the newly enthroned sovereign, after all, was but an opportunistically laicized Buddhist priest who acquired literacy only as an adult!), the latter became so enraged that he wrote these lines in a personal letter to the offender:

> I have received the Mandate of Heaven to lead the Chinese people and drive away the barbarians [that is, the Mongols of the Yuan] in order to bring peace to China. This despite the fact that I came from among the common people, but so did the Han dynasty founder, Kao-tsung [sic., the correct title is Kao-tsu] in antiquity. Hence, it is not permissible for you to neglect my state on the pretext of illness.[58]

Ming Taizu's sentiment expresses dramatically the tension between his newly established regime and one agency of transcendence, deemed necessary to the validity and success of his reign, that nonetheless required pacification and incorporation. It helps explain as well why the worship of one particular human teacher and his disciples, a practice unprecedented in Chinese antiquity, became the recurrent concern in court politics during virtually all dynastic periods from the Song to the Qing. Whereas Mei Fu initially in 8 B.C.E. in his petition was attempting to align the Han, by means of canonizing the descendants of Confucius, with the so-called Three Unities (santong 三統) that pointed to the revered dynasties of antiquity, the language of the Song official Xiong He 熊鉌 identified canonization with the proper transmission of the Way (*daotong* 道統).[59] This change of terms again revealingly discloses how deeply the Confucian literati were invested in the cult, for their own roles and functions in the imperially ordered cosmos were thus implicated and defined. "Preparing for, participating in, and offering sacrifices to the gods and spirits of the imperial pantheon was an integral and important part of being an official."[60] The ritual debates on the minutiae of the action and variation of the canonical members receiving worship that intermittently engaged the emperor's court thus also became tale-telling signs of how Confucianism as asserted court orthodoxy was understood and interpreted during a particular period. Regardless of the vicissitudes of either hermeneutics or ritual, the importance of sacrificing to Confucius and company found eloquent testimony among the rulers themselves. As the Ming emperor Wuzong's formal edict (1509) to the Kong clan in Qufu district had declared, "This [matter of sacrificing to your ancestor] is the noble activity of our nation and not just the glory of your single household 茲惟我國家之盛事，非獨爾一家之榮也 ."[61] To sum up the extraordinary significance of the deified Confucius in cementing religion and a vital part of Chinese statecraft, I can do no better than to quote Huang Chin-hsing's own concluding remark on the subject:

> The Confucian temple was well integrated into the political-cultural system of the Chinese empire. From the T'ang onward, there were only two kinds of worship that were implemented throughout the empire: one, for the gods of land and harvest; and the other, for Confucius. But the cult of Confucius enjoyed higher rites than the gods of land and harvest. Together with royal clan temples (tsung-miao 宗廟) and the worship of Heaven (chi-t'ien 祭天), the Confucian temple stood among the most important ritual institutions for rulers.[62]

4

Daoism:
The Promise of Another Country

WITH THIS UNDERSTANDING of what constitutes the nature
of political authority, founded on an ancient religiosity
that was based in large part on kinship considerations and
funded historically by both the discourse and the rituals of imperial ideology, we can perceive readily both the
seeds and flowering of competition and rivalry, leading to
unavoidable tension and sporadic conflict between the
historical Chinese state and any deviant figure or form of
socio-religious movement.

In terms of the ideology that has been sketched out
thus far, history has shown that Confucianism has contributed the largest share to both its formation and its maintenance as a dominant political discourse and institution
throughout the imperial period. As the previous chapter
has demonstrated, the canonization of the Confucian
lineage and the incorporation of the sage's worship into the
state cult means that salient aspects of Confucianism as a
cultural tradition are irrevocably bound to imperial ritualism. Because the Confucians understand human nature to
be fundamentally a bundle of desires (of preferences and
predilections) that require channeling and discipline, ritual
propriety becomes paramount in their teachings.[1] Doing
the right thing betokens wanting the right thing, and thus
the sovereign on inspection tours, as the quoted passage
of the *Record of Rites* revealingly asserts, must discover
what the people like or dislike. According to the Confucian
ethics of desire, action is a symptom of human subjectivity, variously denominated in classical rhetoric as nature
(*xing*), disposition (*qing*) and heart-and-mind (*xin*), and

this is why performance of a different ritual, or of no ritual, is the same as performing the wrong ritual—a transgression requiring immediate control and rectification.

The formation of didactic discourse and ruling ideology on the part of the official elites on behalf of the state is one thing. As, however, all students of Chinese history and institutions—especially those attending to modern and contemporary developments—realize, the implementation of policies issuing from the central government and how effective and far-reaching that process can be are quite different matters. Social stratifications and recalcitrant regional cultures are only two of several huge factors in preventing easy and successful administration by the centralized state. Throughout China's imperial period since the Han, Confucian learning and the life-long scrutiny of Confucian texts might have been not only the staple pedagogical experience for both men and women; the mastery of such materials also provided the key to the ladder of success for the male population in formal education and officialdom. Nonetheless, even those members of the official elites who succeeded in their careers and writings in establishing a permanent reputation as devout advocates of the Way of Ruism, like Han Yu of the Tang and Ouyang Xiu and Sima Guang of the Song, might in their private and family lives engage in activities contradicted or even condemned by their own "official" and articulated beliefs. Similarly, the person of the emperor could be as ardent a sponsor and promoter of two different religious traditions at the same time (for example, Wendi of the Sui) as he could also be their implacable foe in another era (for instance, Gaozu of the Northern Zhou). In Europe of medieval Christendom, on the other hand, just as it is hard to imagine one Holy Roman Emperor privately engaged in observing the rites of Judaism or Islam, so the notion that an intimate companion of Robin Hood was possibly a Muslim Moor can only exist in the revisionist fantasy of Hollywood. These examples may thus betray a difference of religious conviction and practice that lends validity to the observation by a contemporary Chinese scholar of popular religion(s):

> The Eastern civilization represented by China manifestly differed from the West, and the society erected on the foundation of Confucian thinking diverged in many ways from the Christian tradition in the West. This, however, concerns only one aspect of the matter. The Confucian tradition could not encompass the entire intellectual realm, nor did it have the power to control by itself alone the entire race and act as its guide for the future. [Beyond that tradition], China still had a vast domain of religious culture, and that was the religion that had constituted for the vast majority of the people the point of supporting their life of the spirit and their final refuge to become the central content of human consciousness in that era 正是宗教曾经构成绝大多数人精神生活的支撑点和最後归宿，成为那一时代人类意识的核心内容.[2]

According to Kristofer Schipper, it was the Han elevation of Confucianism to state orthodoxy that opened the gulf between "the state and its administration, the official country," and the different traditions of "the real country, the local structures being expressed in regional and unofficial forms of religion."[3] Historical Daoism, in the self-understanding of the believing community, did not originate in late Han, but its beginning as an "organized religion," so designated by prevalent scholarship, was associated at the time with political unrest and popular uprisings. The military revolt in which the Celestial Master (142 A.D.) and Yellow Turban (182 A.D.) movements were involved would for this reason set the teeth of the central state on edge for much of the duration of Chinese history, including even the present regime. Still, the incipient or explicit conflict that Daoism poses for official state culture has to do much more with alternative interpretations of political authority, social organization, ritual forms, religious functions concerning healing, exorcism, and related activities, and the relations of individual to group or community.

This conflict can appear in the very textual sources on which our knowledge of those early movements depend, as, for example, in the document *Dianlue* 典略 authored by Yu Huan 魚豢, one of the three principal sources from which Chen Shou 陳壽 drew to construct his *History of the Three Kingdoms*. For Chen's biography of Zhang Lu 張魯 (190–220), the "denigrating"[4] description of his grandfather Zhang Ling 張陵 and followers as "rice robbers (*mizei* 米賊)" in another source like the *Hou Hanshu* 後漢書 75 was not only repeated, but the passage by Yu cited in the section immediately following the narrative amplified it to "fiendish robbers (*yaozei* 妖賊)." The use of the word *yao* is significant, if only because its common and pervasive deployment for such a long time in the history of Chinese rhetoric reveals powerfully the predilections and biases of the culture's discursive practice.

The graph's evolved meaning from the notion of feminine seductiveness (so *Shuowen*) to the explicit association with unnatural or supernatural phenomena that are injurious and hurtful renders it almost a buzz word for signifying, from the perspective of accepted orthodxy, all that is *hetero*, all that is fearfully and hostilely other. The string of binomial terms deriving from this word—*yaoyan* 妖言 or beguiling/deviant words, *yaoyi* 妖異 or uncanny manifestations/ beings, *yaoguai* 妖怪 or fiends and imps, *yaobian* 妖變 or fiendish alterations (that is, portents), *yaomo* 妖魔 or fiendish demons, *yaonie* 妖孽 or bogies and accursed beings, *yaoshu* 妖術 or fiendish techniques (like magic, sorcery), *yaoshu* 妖書 or magic writings, *yaojing* 妖精 or fiendish essence (that is, an evil spirit, goblin), and *yaoxie* 妖邪 or fiendish deviancy[5]—informs and studs the discourses of fiction and non-fiction that treat beliefs and practices not having been sanctioned officially. State sponsored sacrifices to deities, ancestors, and apotheosized beings may traffic with the suprahuman or the supernatural, but they are not *yao*. What is not approved or what departs from established norms will run the risk of this disparaging tag, and historically the followers of various popular religions no less than those of Daoism (hence the frequently used *yao Dao* as a derogatory title) and Buddhism (*yao seng* or fiendish monk) have had their share of being so labeled. It is no surprise that the Yu passage cited above continues its editorializing judgment on these leaders of the so-called "Way of the Five Pecks of Rice (*Wudoumi dao* 五斗米道)" and only later changed by believers to the more reverent "Way of the Celestial Masters (*Tianshi dao* 天師道)." Explaining how the movement acquired its name, that the families healed by the followers of Zhang were asked to donate five pecks of rice, Yu Huan thus added a further observation: "They actually were not effective in curing illnesses but only indulged in excessive foolishness. The little people, however, were blind and stupid, and they competed with each other to serve [these masters] 實無益於治病，但為淫妄，然小人昏愚，競共事之."[6] As modern scholars of Daoism realize only too well, objective neutrality, if ever practicable in writing itself or even desirable, was hardly a staunch criterion governing the writing of either history or biography, official or otherwise, in pre-modern Chinese records.

Those records, however, do provide ample and sustained accounts of not merely "little people" swayed by the acts of teachings of different religious leaders and groups. They afford just as richly detailed a chronicle of how the emperors themselves and ministers high and low were deeply engaged in religious activities both prescribed by the established state cult ideology and those fashioned by the idiosyncratic desires of individual rulers. As has been pointed out early in this study, sacrifices led by the ruler in representation of his officials and people were regarded as one of the two "great affairs of state" in classical religion, the other being military expeditions.[7] As the *Classic of Documents* describes the royal duties, "he would make the *lei* sacrifice appropriate to the High *Di*, the *yan* sacrifice for the Six Honored Ones, the *wang* sacrifice to the hills and streams, and then extend such worship to the host of deities."[8] The purpose of such wide-ranging rites, as explicated by ancient theorists, was not simply to benefit the ruler alone, but through his action, the sacrifices, as a Chu minister declares in the *Speeches for the States*, provided "the means to illumine filial piety and calm the citizens, to comfort the nation and pacify the people. They are not to be stopped."[9]

Manifest in such exalted rhetoric is, of course, the venerable ideal running through the length of political culture in China, that the paramount importance of the community or the body politic's well-being should, in especially the principle of the Confucian discourse, dwarf any single individual, including the supreme ruler. Ritual history, on the other hand, tells a signficantly different story to the extent that, as archeological evidence has shown, the matters of the king's health or the severity of his illness often became, in high antiquity already, the topic of divinatory inquiry. Although it may be argued, of course, that the health of the king may vitally affect the welfare of the state, it is also not a preposterous assumption to posit that a desire for personal prosperity and felicity might just as powerfully motivate the most "virtuous and enlightened (賢明)" head of state. The ritual activities undertaken by the sovereign, in other words, may betoken a mixture of compliance with prescribed norms or their wilful defiance, but the emperor's sentiments and behavior are known to posterity only in discursive representation. That representation, even if it is in the form of official historiography, betrays inevitably the vexing doubleness of its nature. Constituted in language, the representation itself unavoidably reflects the mechanical ambiguity inherent in the linguistic sign and its system of signification no less than the manipulation of subjectivity inherent in the acts of writing and reading. Because such manipulation is nevertheless indispensable to the production of meaning, regardless of whether this production is seen from the authorial or readerly perspective, it is nothing if not also an exercise of power. Constituted by language as well, what is represented may not be the actual, intended object of representation as such but only a discursively constituted field of assertion and counter-assertion, by which different persons or social factions implicated in the discourse seek to contest, constrain, or even dominate each other.

This contemporary understanding of discourse[10] may, in turn, help to clarify an obsessive theme in the historiography of the Han—the etiology of disasters and omens (solar eclipses, draught, locust, floods, earthquakes, famines, unseasonable climate, and abnormal epiphanies and manifestations) in conjunction with "emperorship," since proper explanation of portents is deemed crucial to the state's self-understanding of its rule and concern for permanence.[11] Earlier scholars such as Wolfram Eberhard and Zheng Zhiming have tabulated the numerous instances recorded in Ban Gu's *Hanshu* to postulate either the invention of a morally correlative cosmology in which the emperor allegedly was to have played a pivotal role, or the intimate interaction between both political ideals and policies and religious beliefs and rites, whether elite or popular.[12] The official account details repeated edicts that broadcasted imperial self-recriminations in the face of calamities (for example, the confession of personal guilt and oversight) and authorized acts of public relief that included mass computation of jail terms, reduction and temporary exemption of agricultural taxation, and increase of payment to the elderly widows and widowers.[13] A more recent study, however, accentuates how Ban Gu's purported rehearsal of events in the Han court reveals a subterranean "history" of conflict, during which not only rivalling models of the emperor are set forth (one based on Dong Zhongshu's theory of resonance between Heaven and humanity and one based on *Huainanzi*'s notion of "essential sincerity (*jingcheng* 精誠) to move the cosmos"), but the very category of "emperorship" itself is revealed to be "no longer a self-evident entity, but rather a set of complex and dynamic relations."[14] Significantly enough, if the thesis developed by our contemporary scholar is accepted, the two competing models traced out by Wang Aihe would, in fact, point to two traditions that can be unmistakably denominated as Confucian and Daoist respectively. In such a situation stretched out over centuries, "the pivotal position of the emperor in power relations was constantly contested and reproduced through the discursive actions of interpreting omens and theorizing cosmos."[15]

One huge indicator of such discursive action, in fact, may be seen from the Han down through the Period of Disunion in the proliferation of the data appropriate to "interpreting omens and theorizing cosmos." For the elites loyal to Confucian teachings, the Master's refusal to speak of "anomaly, violence, disorder, and spirits 怪力亂神" (*Analects* 7. 20) might have been exemplary taboo to be faithfully observed. The etiology of disasters, on the other hand, deriving from the the sovereign's need for proper response to such disasters, had little choice but to attend to these four topics. Dong Zhongshu (see below) and his fellow Confucians might have pushed hard for the sole orthodoxy of their own tradition, but the correlative cosmology that their own ideas contributed to fashioning only implicated ever more profoundly the emperor's character and action with respect to prodigies and aberrations of all varieties. Such a motivation led eventually to the creation, by documenting from Warring States and Han sources, of "a fairly coherent tradition of cosmographic collection. These ideas and practices [thus collected] were based on a common set of assumptions about the nature of governance and the relation between the royal or . . . imperial center and its social, geographic, even cosmological and spiritual periphery."[16] Part of this tradition also took shape in the specimen of new writing known as "recording anomaly" or "anomaly accounts (zhi guai 志怪)," the purpose of which was to institute control through inclusive narration.

Although this genre of writing has often been regarded as a form of proto-fiction by literary historians, an inquiry from the perspective of the history of religions, as Robert Campany had done, might yield a different interpretation. Anomaly accounts, as his trenchant analysis of their constitutive elements of poetics, logic, rhetoric, and ethics has demonstrated, not only sought to legitimate reflexively such accounts by acknowledging their unavoidable (read historical) occurence past and present adumbrated in canonical sources, but they also revealed the desire to domesticate the strange, the exotic, and the local by prescribing discursive explanation. Threading through this immense body of literature is thus the constant motif of recommending appropriate understanding and response.

> The genre provided a common arena of contention between proponents of divergent—and sometimes directly competing—perspectives on the nature of the world and humanity's place in it, the relationship between what we would call "religion" and "culture," the scope of the ruler's authority, and the nature of certain taxonomic boundaries . . . . [despite] all the fuzziness and porousness of the boundaries between . . . the cluster of Chinese terms translatable as "Daoist," "Buddhist," and "Confucian" . . . . Proponents of each stance were clearly

engaged in a constant struggle for cultural [and political] authority, measured in ways as tangible as favored positions at court and the imperial sponsoring—or else the imperially mandated destruction—of local religious establishments.[17]

Such forms of contestation and reproduction extend, of course, well beyond the Han. If "the way of utmost sincerity," according to the *Doctrine of the Mean* 24, comprises of "the ability to know beforehand 至誠之道，可以前知," such prescience is not merely godlike (故至誠如神), as this Confucian classic pointedly declares, for on the proper knowledge of omens also hangs literally the fate of nations. It thus behooves all rulers and ministers to pay special heed to auguries and their interpretation.[18] The field of contestation, however, is not confined to just the etiology of disasters. The probity of governance that can lead either to the flourishing of the imperial domain or its decline and demise, the stable and core purpose animating official histories acknowledged by all of the imperial period, hinges once more on many aspects of "emperorship" that are discursively presented and debated. In the narrative that runs through volumes, one recurrent aspect appears precisely in the description of how various emperors have acted "religiously." In sum, Chinese historiography, for political and didactic reasons that should be obvious, has been keen in showing to posterity the mode and manner of the emperor's traffic with transcendence, but this traffic is more often than not depicted as an event the nature or desirability of which has been suggested on his subjects's advice, petition, or memorial.

In the imperial era, Qin Shihuangdi inaugurated the tradition with his attributed decision to designate black as his empire's official color in accordance with the emergent theory of the Five Phases. He also was said to have participated in the then popular enterprise common among "the lords of the world" to seek drugs of immortality reputedly available in the three fairy islands of the eastern sea. For these familiar stories, it is important for our argument to notice that the voice and technique of the Grand Scribe are also most consistent. The first mention of the Five Powers' tradition (*wude zhi zhuan* 五德之傳) simply identified the emperor as one who promulgated its use.[19] Characteristic of the *Shiji*'s pattern of overlapping and incremental narration, however, the second account of the same topic offers additional details that may indicate also greater editorial judgment. Having identified the followers of Zou Yan 騶衍 as advocates of "the movement of the Five Powers (*wude zhi yun* 五德之運)," the narrator goes on to point out that "Shihuang made use of the theory because the people of Qi memorialized on it when Qin became emperor 及秦帝而齊人奏之，故始皇采用之."[20] Similarly, the emperor's decision to send "virgin boys and girls to go onto the sea" for the drugs of immortality was, according to the historian's later report, in response to the "countless masters of techniques/methods who had spoken on the matter 方士言之不可勝數."[21] Earlier in the "Basic Annals" section, however, one of those masters is identified as Xu Fu 徐市, another person from the region of Qi.[22]

These episodes have often been regarded as evidence revealing the emperor's inclination towards religion or "superstition," enhanced by the fact that the narrative contains numerous other episodes depicting Shihuangdi in this manner. The ruler is said to be fond of divination through dreams and other omens.[23] Responding to a prophecy couched in esoteric writings with magical illustrations (*tulu* 圖錄) that "Hu [possibly a convenient reference to barbarians] would be the one to overthrow the Qin," the emperor immediately dispatched a general with three hundred thousand troops to attack "Hu and invade the region of Henan."[24] Listening to a certain Lu Sheng from the state of Yan and his description of "the perfected person (*zhenren* 真人)," who can "enter water without drowning and fire without burning, [who] astride the nebulose air will endure with Heaven and Earth" (an all too apparent quotation of *Zhuangzi* 6 conflated with ch. 1), the emperor replied: "I love this perfected person! From now on, I'll not use the royal 'We' and refer to myself only as the perfected person."[25] Not only does Sima Qian the narrator plainly remark that "Shihuang hated the mention of death so much that his various officials dared not speak of any matter concerning death,"[26] but the ruler's excesses, so he also reports, eventually alienated even the "technicians" who served him in these matters. Before Hou Sheng (= Hou Gong of an earlier passage?) and Lu Sheng fled his service, they thus reached this judgment of the emperor: "He is so covetous of authority and power that we should not seek for him the drugs of immortality."[27]

As one who could justly boast of so many stupendous accomplishments, including the unprecedented act of consolidating in one empire—through conquest and policy—the huge domain of warring territories of centuries, how could Qin Shihuang suffer the complete loss and ruin of what he had gained so quickly? This question, of course, has been posed in countless ways and times down through the centuries. The initial judgment of the Grand Scribe himself appears, with a masterly stroke of rhetorical mediation, in the voice of Jia Yi's famous indictment of Qin's moral and political failings, reproduced at great length at the end of the "Qin Basic Annals" with the historian's explicit endorsement and praise. As most subsequent commentators of the so-called "Guo Qin lun 過秦論" have observed, Jia's elaborate critique may be summed up in one key sentence, that the Qin ruler, despite the enormity of his newly acquired power and the strength of his military might, "did not enact benevolence and justice 仁義不施."[28] The concrete substance of this charge finds expression in the litany of the emperor's faults, that

with a base and covetous mind he exercised the cunning
of self-aggrandisement; that he neither trusted meritorious
subjects nor loved his own people; that he abolished the
Kingly Way and established private power in its stead; that he
proscribed cultural writings and made more severe the penal
codes; that he preferred deception and violence over benevolence and justice; that he resorted to tyranny and cruelty as
the font of empire. [29]

Readers may be interested to notice that his indictment
never mentioned anything about the emperor's person or
polity that remotely intimates his dalliance with the occult,
the supernatural, or the religious. Jia Yi's critique, and the
Grand Scribe's unambiguous endorsement thereof, have
been aptly received in posterity as a classic statement of
"Confucian" judgment, but the judgment so conceived must
be understood in terms of both the recorded censure and
the ironical contrast posed by the narrated details. How
would a reader committed to a Confucian point of view re-
act to the emperor's fondness for the activities promoted by
the "technicians" and the ideals of "the perfected person"?
Is Sima Qian's meticulous identification of the geographical
origin of such "technicians" itself a reflection of the tension, observed by Schipper earlier in this section, between
"the official country" newly enlarged and diversified by
conquered territories and "the local structures expressed in
regional and unofficial forms of religion"?

These are no idle or far-fetched questions, because as
modern scholarship of Daoism has demonstrated, *zhenren*
and *fangshi* are only two of the several other terms and
categories inextricably embedded in the historical discourse of Daoism, despite the fact that the historian's dates
(145–*ca.* 85 B.C.E.) antedate the formal rebellious beginnings
of organized Daoism by almost two centuries.[30] This is not
so much a suggestion for acknowledging an earlier date for
the existence of Daoism, a highly ambiguous *terminus a quo*

given our present state of scholarly knowledge, as it is an observation on how terms of personalities, practices, and professions not easily assimilable into the state cult system have nevertheless entered the discursive fabric of canonical history. Their presence and interaction with the highest echelons of imperial government receive continual notice in the official narratives, for their impact provides also a consistent contest and contrast to the evolving development of asserted state orthodoxy. Few descriptions can rival the terseness of the little tale tucked in Sima Qian's narration of the newly crowned Han ruler's penchant in creating and co-opting divine potency by fiat. The first emperor Gaozu (r. 206–194 B.C.E.), fresh from a military victory during the second year of his reign, was questioning his subjects on how many *Di*s were worshipped in antiquity. Informed that there were sacrifices established for four such deities classified by the colors of white, blue, yellow, and red, he said,

> "I have heard that there are five *Di*s in Heaven. Why are there only four?" When none knew how to answer the question, Gaozu made this declaration: "I know it! They were waiting for me to install the fifth one 乃待我而具五也." Whereupon he established the Black *Di*, and named the place for his worship Shrine of the North. . . .[In addition], he issued the following proclamation: "I value greatly sacrifices and revere the offerings. Now the offerings to the Exalted *Di* and the sacrifices that various gods of mountains and rivers should receive must each be performed as the timely rituals of old."[31]

Reading such an episode, one finds it difficult not to think about the making of ancestors or the canonization of Confucius and his descendants that we have discussed previously. The point about China's imperial power, it seems, is not to encourage separating the realms of the sacred from the profane, the divine from the human, the religious from the secular, as any modern student is instructed to learn from the history of Western Europe and the medieval Church's theory of the two kingdoms and their two keys respectively. For the Chinese emperor, his claim to transcendence (his name, after all, is already Gaozu or Gaodi, High Ancestor or High *di*) derives from creating and incorporating transcendence, an act that is at once indivisibly religious and political. This predilection and policy continued through much of the Han, as indicated by the words of one imperial command issued by Wendi (r. 179–156 B.C.E.):

> Since we assumed the throne thirteen years ago, we have till now been indebted to the efficaciousness of our ancestral temples and the blessings bestowed by the Gods of Soil and Grain. All within our borders have been prosperous and secure, and the citizens have been free from illness. Good harvests have increased with the years. How could we, a person of no virtue, enjoy this? These are the gifts of the Exalted *Di* and the various spirits. Now we have heard that he whose virtue had been rewarded would recompense the merit of the giver. We would, therefore, increase the sacrifices to the various spirits.[32]

When we reach the lengthy reign of Han Wudi (r. 140–86 B.C.E.), the time current to the Grand Scribe himself, the narration seems to dwell on no other topic except the religious concerns and activities of successive rulers. For good reason, therefore, the narrator begins his story of Wudi with the most succinct characterization: "He especially revered the sacrifices to ghosts and spirits 尤敬鬼神之祀."[33] Because the historian himself had accompanied the emperor on some of his sacrificial tours, Sima Qian's terminal remark in this section of his narrative emphasizes his own participation in such activities and his personal observances on the purported actions by the *fangshi* and sacrificial officials. Leaving the rehearsal of ritual materials and utensils to officials charged with such matters, he said,

"I have written down upon retirement all that I knew of the service to ghosts and spirits since antiquity, making a thorough presentation of the outisde and inside of such affairs. Gentlemen of all posterity will have it for their perusal."[34]

Since this section of the *Shiji* is titled the "Treatise on the *Feng* and *Shan*," the content aptly focuses on what past rulers down to those current in the author's era have done with these two named rituals. According to Sima Qian's grandiloquent rhetorical opening of his treatise, their performative observance has been linked intimately with dynastic glory and their disuse with decline. The historian's meticulous narration of these rituals and related activities through the different imperial generations thus also validates their perceived capacity for securing allegedly the legitimacy and stability of an emperor's reign. Despite Sima Qian's own stated understanding, however, his narrative also presents ironically some startling variations of interpretation that again reflect variant views and altered procedures promoted by others, many of whom were hardly the bureaucrats duly in charge of official rituals.

Returning to the account of Han Wudi, we may notice the emperor's fondness for consulting with *fangshi* and other ritual masters has won for their counsel and advice extensive recording in the narrative. One Li Shaojun reached an audience with the Throne by advocating sacrifices to the Stove (to facilitate eventual alchemical operations), the Way of Grains, and the Method for Resisting Age, but he also suggested an even loftier aim for the *Feng-Shan* rites with these words to the emperor:

> Sacrificing to the Stove will bring forth certain creatures. Bringing forth certain creatures can transform cinnabar into gold. Using food and drink utensils made from such gold will prolong your age. When your age is prolonged, then you will be able to see the immortals living on the isle Penglai in the

sea. The one who saw them and performed the *Feng-Shan* to attain a deathless condition was none other than the Yellow Emperor.[35]

Even a beginning student of Chinese religions should be able to tell that what Mr. Li championed had far more to do with the practices espoused squarely by Daoism (for example, alchemy, dietary observance, the quest for physical longevity) than with the Confucianism of the state cult. In Sima's narration, Wudi appears apparently as such a believer of emergent Daoist doctrines already that, even after Li Shaojun died of illness, the emperor "only supposed that he had been transformed and departed, not died 以為 化去不死." Such ardent faith could not be sustained without its own reward, and the emperor's persistent quest for the drugs and human agents of immortality, as the narrator sarcastically remarks, "only brought even more strange and crooked *fangshi* from the coastal regions of Yan and Qi to come to speak to him about the services to spirits."[36]

Shiji's portrait of such a ruler whose interest and energy seem bent only on exploring the occult and the esoteric arts, however, should not be taken as complete, for various parts of an equally impressive work of official history, the *Hanshu*, confronts us with quite a different picture. Consistent with his known critique of Sima Qian for over reliance on Daoist perspectives, Ban Gu's extended representation of Wudi gives us a ruler whose mind and administrative abilities are hardly devoid of intelligence, industry, and rationality. Wudi's reign from ancient official history and modern historiography both provide us with accounts of extensive accomplishments in economic and commercial developments, structural reform and addition of governmental bureaus, agricultural expansion, diplomatic initiatives with territories both east and west of the Han domain, and repeated military excursions.[37] Most germane to the theme of the present study concerns, of course, his attitude and behavior towards religions.

The famous "Dialogical Discussion of Policy (*dui ce* 對策)," the text of which takes up almost all of the biography of his equally famous minister, Dong Zhongshu 董仲舒 (179–*ca.* 104 B.C.E.), begins with the ruler's admission to "constant rumination on how to secure an empire of ten thousand generations 永惟 [思] 萬世之統" as the cause for assembling his worthy counselors for open discussion. This anxiety of endurance, so to speak, is hardly peculiar to this particular emperor, for the "Qin Basic Annals" already had shown us a similarly poignant depiction of Shihuangdi. The text of Wudi's initial charge and query, devoted largely and understandably to surveying the vicissitudes of previous dynasties (for example, why did some ancient rulers have to work harder than others?) and what can be learned from their rise and fall, climaxes in the demand for cogent answers for such questions as the following:

> If the Three Dynasties had received the Heavenly Mandate, where is the talismanic evidence? What is the origin giving rise to the changes brought by disasters and alterations? The essential conditions of nature and life may be short-lived or lengthy; they may be kindly or base. It is a common practice to hear of their names but their principles have not been illumined.[38]

On the face of the emperor's language, these questions seem primed for probing philosophical and even metaphysical matters relative to securing, of course, the future of his dynasty. Characteristic of his life-long devotion to the study of the Confucian legacy crystallized for him in the *Spring-and-Autumn Annals*, Dong replies with essentially a series of exegetical exposition of Confucian dicta liberally supported by allusions to Mencius and especially to Xunzi. The central thrust of the minister's disquisition articulates powerfully a Confucian understanding of *xing* (nature) and *qing* (disposition, desires), both of which, if political order is to be maintained, are to be regulated and refined by the paideia of inherited cultural forms of history, poetry, music, and ritual, all cherished institutions by now of the Confucian tradition. It touches on virtually nothing catering to what we have seen as possibly the emperor's religious predilections. With the ruler peppering the minister with further queries, the argumentative exchange proceeds in such fashion until it reaches the grand summation submitted by Dong at the very end:

> The great uniformity of principles achieved in the *Spring-and-Autumn* is the constant web of Heaven and Earth, the rectitude shared by antiquity and the present [reading 通誼 as 通義]. Now if you followed a different path and used a person of different persuasion, then there would be diverse formulas from a hundred clans/schools (*jia*), and all their references would be dissimilar. Therefore, the sovereign above would have no means to maintain the uniformity of principles, and when codes and institutions changed severally, those below would not know what to adhere to. Your simple subject, therefore, proposes that whatever not included within the curriculum of the Six Arts and the method of Confucius should have its Way abolished and its equal presentation [for your hearing] prohibited. Only when deviant and wayward propositions have been extinguished can principles and records become one and the laws and norms comprehensible. Then the people would know what to obey.[39]

Because Dong's suggestion was indeed adopted by Wudi eventually, the minister attained immortal credit for instigating successfully the installation of Confucianism as state orthodoxy. The historical record itself, however, proffers a much more complicated and protracted process, carried out in consultative and disputative assembly of a number of high officials over several years. There were similar proposals by different officials championing the Confucian cause to "abolish the hundred schools," and they were met with resistance by others, including the Queen Mother Lady Dou who allegedly showed obvious preference for Daoist causes. Dong Zhongshu finally succeeded only when the Queen Mother Dou had died.[40] However we may finally assess Dong's impact on Wudi's policies, the vital linkage between imperial governance and forms of religious convictions and actions cannot be questioned. "By taking part in the established cults, and by inaugurating some new rites," writes Michael Loewe, "Wu-ti was serving the interests of the state and the growth of empire in a manner that was peculiarly reserved for him as emperor and denied to other mortals. As the supreme arbiter of human destinies on earth, he was taking steps to forge a link with the sacred powers in the hope of securing their protection and blessing."[41]

Loewe's succinct description of Wudi's motive for ritual performance applies equally to other emperors, for as the scholar's account makes abundantly clear, the exigencies of history—the cost of maintaining religious services, the problem of distance and geographical location for cultic sites and shrines, the number of services that may vary with the economy and state expenditure, the availability of personnel (including migrant workers) to undertake ceremonial labor, and the reformation of the rituals themselves deriving from variant interpretations—include both material and human factors that confront every ruler concerned in securing the future of the state.[42] Nevertheless, the interesting phenomenon we have witnessed in this cursory examination of two of the most illustrious early emperors of China is that there were other religious elements at play in their court and in their empire that worked to produce a twofold ironic development relative to the Chinese ruler's protracted fascination with religious Daoism—with its practices and the sundry personnalities in different dynasties that have sought to win favor and power from him, his extended clan and his court.

First, Daoist doctrines, though unintended to be received in such manner, actually help revert the divinized ruler of the Confucian discourse into a mere mortal. If in the state cult ideology the emperor must fulfil religious obligations "denied to other mortals," the ironic allure of Daoism even at this incipient stage of development stems from the religion's potent address to the problem of mortality that no emperor can avoid. The promised transcendence in Daoist discourse and practice—health (including youthfulness, stamina, and fertility pledged upon respiratory exercises, dietary rituals, and sexual gymnastics), physical longevity, miraculous powers and procedures in inducing physical transformations, healing (herbal medications and pharmaceutics, *qigong*, exorcism), the state of deathlessness—thus makes for a poignant contrast to the exalted titles that Confucians discursively and routinely confer on the ruler, especially the founding emperor of a new dynasty. Variously named *Gaozu, Gaozong, Taizong, Taizu,* and *Di,* the wretched man must till cope with the fears and desires common to all mortals, but in the case of the emperor, those affects unite both his personal and vocational concerns. He is driven to live out the sardonic Chinese adage—"after becoming emperor he would wish for ascension as an immortal 做得皇帝想升仙"—because the quest for permanence as a desideratum for his reign is not limited only to his person. It extends from him to his immediate household members, his eventual descendants, and his extended clan, all of whom contributing to the constitution of his entire dynasty.

What renders such contrast ever a subversive challenge to the claims of imperial sovereignty is that the promised transcendence of Daoism, by its very principle, must be a democratic promise. The fruits of cultivating the Dao are available to humans of every stratum imaginable, but their secret formulas and recipes (hence *fang* 方 and *jue* 訣) belong to another canon and another tradition. Reversing the social hierarchy asserted and institutionalized by the Confucian discourse, the Dao in Laozi "images the forebears of *Di* 象帝之先" (*Daodejing* 4).[43] Followers of this Dao or its variant interpretation thus may always exacerbate the religio-political tension between "the official country" and the unofficial "local structures" that, in countless occasions of China's long history, has led to open dissension and armed conflict.

The second ironic effect wrought by developed doctrines of religious Daoism points to another paradoxical phenomenon discernible in discursive metaphors and organizational structures of transcendence from those sponsored by the state cult. Students of Daoism and of popular religions have often pointed out how the developed pantheon of the tradition virtually models a form of imperial government, with a huge and motley crew of hierarchically differentiated deities (local, regional, euhemeristically canonized officials, and foreign gods and demons incorporated from Buddhism and even Hinduism) presided by a Jade Emperor at the top. This represents, as Stephan Feuchtwang rightly observes,

> a conception of authority which is at the centre of the apparent replication of imperial authority. . . . The practices of popular religion, the imperial state cults and the Daoist rites provide alternative lines of reference through the same cosmology. In Daoism, but not in the system of state rites, the categories of the cosmology are applied as real forces directly upon immediate circumstances. In the imperial rites, the hierarchical and resonant structure of a moral-physical universe was displayed and anthropomorphisied in representations of historically exemplary individuals [for example, like Confucius], celebrated in official cults. But the gods in popular

temples, though they represent historical persons, are also manifestations of current power to heal and to exorcise.[44]

Astute as Feuchtwang's observation is, there is a further distinction between Daoism and popular religions, because "the real forces" applied directly "upon immediate circumstances" as envisaged by the discrete religious tradition itself—despite its frequent alliance with many of the so-called popular religions—are galvanized and harnessed fundamentally from an interior cosmos of the human body that also is said to mirror the entire natural universe. If the state cult feeds on imperial metaphors that tend to literalize material or geographical reality—mountains and rivers (*shanhe*) as empire, soil and grain (*sheji*) as domain—Daoism thrives in metaphoricity that somatizes and internalizes country and state. As the early medieval theorist of alchemy, Ge Hong 葛洪 (283–343), famously declares in one of the texts most seminal to Daoist beliefs and practices,

> the body of a human individual is the image of a state. The positions of chest and abdomen are like palaces and halls. The ordered display of the four limbs are like the scenes of the countryside. The differentiated bones and joints are like the hundred officials. The spirit is like the ruler, the blood is like the subjects, and the pneumatic vitality is like the citizens. Therefore, he who knows how to govern the body will know how to love the state. One who loves the citizens would want to secure the state; thus one who nourishes his pneumatic vitality [a pointed allusion to the Mencian notion of *yang qi* that now is given a completely different meaning] would preserve his body. When the citizens disperse the state will perish; when the pneumatic vitality exhausts itself, the body will die.[45]

This amazing passage confronts the literal emperor with some very familiar terms such as the state (*guo*), palace and halls (*gongshi*), hundred officials (*bai guan*), ruler (*jun*), and citizens (*min*), but as any reader can see, their meaning is completely displaced in the running series of similes. The potent paradox is thus all too apparent: he who is already the Son of Heaven and the unique lord of an empire is challenged to learn to rule another country. The "cultivation of the self or body (*xiu shen* 修身)" is a term of immense resonance for Confucian disciples because it bespeaks the life-long commitment to moral self-examination and ordering. In Daoist thinking, however, that difficult process betokens an even more arduous and even treacherous undertaking whereby one must do battle with gods and demons resident in one's own frame. Before such thinking received a tremendous boost in the dramatic escalation of internal or physiological alchemy during the Tang, however, the attempt at tapping into the promised resources of the "interior landscape" of one's body may also involve the utilization of pharmaceutical aid of all varieties.

When one examines the official histories of the imperial period, one may be astounded to see how many Chinese emperors had been recorded to have had extensive contacts with Daoist "technicians (*fangshi*)" and the variety of "methods of cultivation (*fangshu*)" that they advocated. Even more arresting would be the number of rulers who perished from ingesting "drugs of immortality." Extant documents indicate, for example, that Cao Cao 曹操 (155–220), founding emperor of the Wei, and his literary sons all had the policy of inviting *fangshi* to the court and practiced such esoteric rituals as "nourishing one's nature" and the use of medical substances.[46] According to the *History of Jin*, Emperor Ai 哀帝 or Sima Pi (r. 362–65) "consistently was devoted to the teachings of Huang-Lao; he abstained from a diet of grain and ingested the drug of immortality. When he took too much, he was poisoned and became completely insentient."[47] Emperor Daowu 道武帝 (386–409) of the Northern Wei (386–534), a reputed supporter of both Buddhism and Daoism, nevertheless was so ardent in his quest for efficacious drugs of immortality that he instituted a special government bureau for the process of refining herbs and chemicals. When the drugs were made, they would first be fed to convicts on death row. This precautionary measure did not prevent the ruler's death later from the poison of a certain "Chilly Stone Powder (寒石散)."[48] The Tang's extensive support of religious Daoism also resulted in the largest number of emperors—including Taizong (627–49), Xianzong (806–821), Muzong (821–25), Jingzong (825–27), Wuzong (841–47), and Xuanzong (847–60)—who died or suffered irremediable poisoning from taking elixir drugs.[49]

If this history of Chinese emperors' involvement with certain aspects of Daoism reveals another *religious* dimension of imperial politics, one that aims at the quest for personal and dynastic permanence not satisfactorily explained or guaranteed by the Confucian discourse, the ironic reverse of such a situation is also apparent. Despite the Daoist emphasis of other-worldly reclusivity (for example, *dunshi* 遁世, *guiyin* 歸隱) as an ideal setting for somatic cultivation, the lust for this-worldly power and prominence is manifest in many of the most celebrated religious figures and leaders of this tradition. Among the early Daoist masters who had experienced extensive involvement with court life and politics, one could name, for example, Lu Xiujing 陸修靜 (406–477), the leader of the Southern School of Celestial Masters, who was honored by imperial summons and solicitations repeatedly from Emprors Wendi (453) and Mingdi (466) of the Song in the Disunion period; his student Tao Hongjing 陶弘景 (456–536), the prodigious scholar of the Maoshan school of medieval Daoism and systematizer of the Shangqing tradition's core texts, who was nicknamed "Prime Minister of the Mountains 山中宰相" because Wudi of the Liang constantly sought his counsel for almost twenty years (505–525) while Tao was practicing austeries; and

Kou Qianzhi 寇謙之 (365–448), the influential reformer of the Northern School of Celestial Masters who, on the support of his friend and patron Cui Hao 崔浩,[50] succeeded in promoting this form of Daoism as virtually a state religion under Emperor Taiwu (424–52) of the Northern Wei.

As we had noted earlier in this section, the precursors of the religious Daoists under the name of technical masters in Qin-Han times could not themselves have been without political ambition. Like the Confucians or any other aspiring state counselors who wanted to make their presence felt or needed at court, the daunting challenge they faced, exemplified in the recorded deliberations of Qin Shihuangdi's courtiers, was to decide whether they were supporting a winner or loser, "an enlightened lord (*mingzhu* 明主)" or "a precarious lord (*weizhu* 危主)."[51] If, as Hou Sheng and Lu Sheng had determined that their emperor was, or had become in the course of time, the latter variety, they could leave imperial service or they might be tempted to cast their support with someone deemed as the rising star. Herein we can readily discern not merely that political ambition often leads to dissent and revolt in the history of Chinese politics, but also that such revolt routinely labeled by historians and sociologists as popular uprising frequently resorts to a religious, even a theological, rhetoric to justify its action.

In the light of the state cult ideology, the Han idealization of the sage dynasties of China's high antiquity, especially the Zhou, means also that rulers and officials could not dodge the concerns relative to "the morally correct transfer of power and for the maintenance of power through dynastic virtue."[52] Unfortunately for the ruling elites, the ancient term, Mandate of Heaven (*tianming* 天命), that supposedly addresses these concerns by distilling the essential meaning of the process had never received a precise definition on the manner and mode of the mandate's transmission. The well-known allowance, on the part of a Confucian thinker like

Mencius, for political insurgents to execute even an unjust tyrant only spawns the added thorny question of when and how regicide may be justified. As a certain Huang Sheng declared during a debate in the court of Emepror Jingdi (156–40 B.C.E.), "Tang [of the Shang] and Wu [of the Zhou] did not receive the Mandate, and therefore their action [in disposing the respective Shang rulers] was murder 湯武 非受命，乃弒也."[53] Like the Calvinist Puritans who would love to believe that they were among those predestined to eternal salvation, the Chinese emperors and the ministers in his service were thus understandably anxious, as it were, to "make their calling and election sure." This nervousness could have led to the circulation of such ideas as the "talismanic verification of the Mandate (*fuming* 符命)"[54] and the "renewed reception of the Mandate (*zai shouming* 再授 命)"[55] fomenting in Han politics. It might have generated in opportunistic dissidents the seditious slogan attributed to Zhang Jue 張角, founder of the Yellow Turbans movement that revolted against the Han in 184: "The Pale Heaven had perished but the Yellow Heaven should be established. The year has arrived at *jiazi* [the binomial term for the first year of the sixty-year cycle of the calender happened to have alighted on 184], and great auspiciousness presides in the empire."[56] The slogan's appeal is replicated in the often cited story from the early parts of the *Daozang* about one legendary Li Hong 李弘 of the fifth century described as a restive rebel. Nothing was said about his qualifications other than the rhetorical mystery of his claim deriving entirely from the prophecy based on anagrammatical dissection of his name to the graphs of *mu zi gong kou* 木子弓口. Apparently, this pithy combination was so effective and potent a sign that both secular history and Daoist scriptures record numerous individuals using the name in political revolt.[57]

The linguistic and rhetorical peculiarities associated with these early Daoist figures and movements undeniably highlight for us again the intimate fusion of religion and politics. Whether it is seen in a focused segment of one or two dynastic periods or over a long stretch of imperial history, religion arguably has been constantly enlisted either to strengthen and bolster the legitimacy of an existing regime or to provide a rallying cause for justifying rebellion. Indeed, the history of the earliest movements associated with the formation of what scholars have come to name as religious Daoism reads like a history of popular uprising, but revolt was often dialectically related to imperial interest and dalliance with the very practices and doctrines espoused by the dissenting communities. In the middle of the second century, enthusiasm generated by the reported epiphany of a divinized Laozi reached such a peak that the emperor Huandi 桓帝 both sent envoys to the countryside to offer sacrifices to the apotheosized sage and established a shrine for him within his own palace (165–66). In 147 and 154, clan groups with the surname of Li 李, the reputed name of the Laozi, rebelled with troops, the second of which installed themselves as Emperor in Sichuan.[58]

We have already alluded above to Zhang Jue of the Yellow Turban fame, who also arose in armed rebellion in 184. Though Zhang was said to have proclaimed the Way of Great Peace 太平道 as a platform for his movement, his career was anything but peaceful. In the detailed narrative on his movement and its suppression recorded in the biography of Huangfu Song 皇甫嵩 (*Hou Hanshu* 101), Jue and his two brothers Bao 寶 and Liang 梁 at their height apparently had tens of thousands of followers, who were also organized into thirty-six military units designated as *fang* 方. Whether the name was chosen as a deliberate parody of the more entrenched meaning of *fang* as a delimited region of clan is not known, but the big unit would number over ten thousand persons, while the smaller units, six or seven thousand. Appointed Defender of the Left 左都尉 by the emperor Lingdi 靈帝 (r. 168–89), Huangfu and other military commanders led Han troops to attack the rebels. The protracted campaign lasting nearly a year provided grim statistics for canonical history that would be similarly noted in past and future records. When Huangfu's army, joined by the forces of Cao Cao, first routed Zhang's troops, the narrative says that "they cut off several tens of thousand heads 斬首數萬級." When Zhang Liang, the brother, was killed, "thirty thousand heads were cut off and those forced to drown in the river reached fifty thousand." Still later, when the brother Zhang Bao was defeated, he was beheaded along with "a hundred thousand plus persons 十餘萬人." More fortunate perhaps than all these followers of his who had lost their lives, Zhang Jue himself was said to have died of illness. According to the *Hou Hanshu*, however, his coffin was dug up and opened so that his severed head could be sent to the imperial capital.

At the beginning of this section, we have also mentioned Zhang Lu, the grandson of the putative founder of the Celestial Masters tradition pejoratively labeled "The Way of the Five Pecks of Rice" in canonical history ("The Biography of Zhang Lu" in *Sanguo zhi* 8). Active for almost three decades in the south-central region of Hanzhong, the government Zhang Lu eventually established was essentially a theocracy, a state that sought, aptly put in the modern Chinese phrase, "to unite government and religion 政教合一." The organization of his government, according to contemporary scholarship, apparently followed a hierarchical pattern set down in the *Classic of Great Peace* 太平經, wherein lay believers were subordinate to such ascending ranks of the clergy as libationers, chief-libations, and the lord-master. Combining religious rituals (confessions of sins, penitential good works like road-building) and compassionate government (erection of hostels for travellers, lightening the penal code, prohibiting reckless taking of life), his government was said to have been welcomed by both Han populace and ethnic nationals.

Despite its reputed attractiveness, however, such an administration, to the extent that it did not profess submission to the Han dynasty, was itself also subject to the other restive forces eager to displace the imperial rule. In 215, the escalating ambition of Cao Cao led to his invasion of Hanzhong with an army of 100,000, crushing the momentary resistance fielded by Zhang's brother, Zhang Heng. Retreating into Sichuan, Zhang Lu quickly decided to spurn surrendering to Liu Bei 劉備 (ostensibly the legitimate heir to the Han throne) and, after three months, submitted instead to Cao Cao, the pretender who would in due course succeed in becoming the founder of the Wei Dynasty. Zhang was rewarded with two titles, the enfeoffment of his five sons, and the betrothal of one of his daughters to one of Cao's sons.[59] His enjoyment of this new found elevation was short lived and possibly very limited, for he died in the following year of 216. Moreover, the political control exerted by Cao Cao over Zhang's clan and followers was both efficient and brutal. When Cao returned north after his conquest, Zhang and his family with their retainers were taken north by the victors as well. Canonical history in different places documented notably the repeated use of forced migration, such that the population of Hanzhong ("several tens of thousand households 數萬戶" in one instance, and "eighty thousand plus persons 八萬餘口" in another)[60] was compelled to trek north for re-settlement three times in a period of four years.[61] Such a move, in fact, may be regarded as part of a larger policy of "suppression through controlled settlement 聚而禁之" specifically developed by Cao Cao towards the technicians (*fangshi*).[62]

Other noted examples in this era of political rebellion associated with the Daoist tradition include the group of several thousand persons led by Celestial Master Chen

Rui 陳瑞 in Sichuan. They were active for more than a year (276–77) before Chen was executed by the Regional Inspector of Yizhou, Wang Jun 王濬.[63] Another rebel Zhang Chang 張昌, a leader of Man ethnic minority, started to assemble as followers in 303 those people who resented the Western Jin government's military draft in connection with its suppression of the uprising of the Li Clan (see below). His uprising in An Lu of the modern Hubei gathered several thousand persons. Because he outfitted his troops with maroon turbans decorated with feathers and claimed to have received "pearl studded robes, jade seals, iron vouchers, and gold drums from Heaven," modern scholarship tends to associate him with the Celestial Master movement.[64] At the height of his success, Zhang managed to capture five prefectures of the lower Yangtze region, but in the end, government forces of the Western Jin sent to suppress (*zhenya* 鎮壓) him triumphed, and "his head was sent to the capital."[65]

Our final example of political revolt associated with formative Daoism is to be found in one Li Te 李特 and his extended family.[66] His grandfather Li Hu 李虎 was already said to have followed the practice of the Celestial Master tradition led by Zhang Lu. Understandably, when Zhang submitted to Cao Cao, Li led some five hundred households to do the same. Cao moved them to the Ba Shu (that is, Sichuan) region and the Lis continued to practice their religion. The Sima clan members who defeated the Wei (Cao's dynasty) and founded the Jin, in their quest for legitimacy for the new regime, were ruthless in their attempt to silence pro-Wei loyalists. During the reign of Huidi 惠帝 (290–305), the government was said to be "in disarray," and the people in regions near Sichuan, suffering intensely from famines caused by locusts and ineffectual administration, resorted to selling their children. When migrant refugees who fled to Sichuan were threatened to have their leaders executed and forcibly removed to their home counties by Jin officials, the people revolted, choosing Li Te as their leader.

Making a sort of religious and political covenant with the people—on the three conditions that they set up monetary loans for the needy, appoint good persons for offices, and strictly obey the revolutionary government—Li soon took portion of the city of Chengdu in 303. Though he later died in battle when Jin forces counter-attacked, his son Li Xiong 李雄 fought on, capturing the rest of Chengdu, and declared himself king in 304. The following year, he was crowned emperor and named his country Dacheng 大成. The story of Li and his uncles' protracted struggle to keep their state alive, with the crucial and efficient assistance by a Daoist named of Long-life Fan (Fan Changsheng 范長生) is too lengthy and complex to be fully recounted here. Despite the relentless battles waged by the government forces and the appalling privations besetting the rebel forces, the Lis managed to retain their state for over three decades before they were finally overthrown in 347. The recognition of their effective government and popular support by both ethnic minorities and Han populace, duly recorded in the *Jinshu*, justified also the verdict of a contemporary scholar: "On the whole, the people of Sichuan fared better under the Lis than the inhabitants of most other parts of China at that time. This was the result of the talents of the Li family founders, the wisdom of their advisors, and the tenets of their religious faith."[67]

Our brief rehearsal of some noteworthy instances of revolt associated with early Daoism should make apparent at least two implications relative to the vicissitudes of religious traditions in Chinese history. The first concerns the entrenched myth, still ardently embraced by many Chinese intellectuals, that there had not been, allegedly, any serious conflict or warfare in Chinese history induced by religion. That conclusion is usually based on the conviction that no large scale *international* conflict principally motivated by religious concerns such as the crusades or the Thirty Years War occurred within China's long political history. Such a view of the matter, however, is susceptible to challenge and even modification if one considers, for example, the prevalent condition of the Disunion Period, when the various warring states or kingdoms in a culturally, geographically, and ethnically fragmented China engaged in intermittent armed conflict based, among other causes, on the explicit clash of religious allegiances. Nor can the uprisings, such as those associated with the formation of early Daoism, be classified as simply the manifestation of local and indigenous political disturbance that eventually found some sort of "legitimate" resolution. The rebels themselves no less than the official governmental forces sent to suppress them, as we have just witnessed, both resorted to patent violence: war was real war—whether its scale was small or large, whether its site was local or regional, and whether the eventual result was the execution of a few leaders or the decapitation of several thousand recalcitrant followers of "unorthodox" practices and beliefs. If a revolt was successful, the regime change would, in fact, establish a new dynasty, and its acceptance would also win eventual canonization in official history. If a revolt was crushed, as, say, the followers of Zhang Jue and his two brothers, their defeat and demise would be chronicled as political disorder pacified (*ping luan* 平亂) or suppressed (*zhenya*) by legitimate forces (read, troops loyal to the imperium). Such rhetoric of canonical historiography, however, should not thereby obscure for us the frequent religious basis of the rebels' action, or the historical repetition of this form of religio-political violence from antiquity to the events of the Taiping Rebellion and beyond. The immensity of suffering and loss of human lives thus incurred surely give the lie to the naive and self-deluding conlusion that, because there was no such religious war, the Chinese as a people have been religiously more tolerant.[68]

The second implication is dialectically related to the first, in that the actual failures in ethics and politics on the part of the ruling classes and the real sufferings and discontent of the people in any particular era or locality provided ample justification for political revolt. What ironically united both rulers and rebels in many instances was the stubborn, ancient belief in the correlation between government and the semiology of its efficacy. It is, therefore, important for us to remember in this connection that one prominent platform of the state cult ideology—that the behavior and character of the sovereign manifest in his governance can be tallied "religiously," by natural and cosmic signs—received firm subscription by all three principal religious traditions of China since the Han. This conviction thus may assist in accounting for both the motivation of the rebels throughout history to rise up against the Chinese state in the name of religion by appealing to esoteric slogans and revelatory prodigies and the state's equally firm commitment to assert and enforce ritual rectitude as well as to control variant religious institutions and their teachings through active engagement and regulation. Court officials, for example, could not have avoided noticing the proliferation in the early medieval period of the so-called books of occult prophecy or prognosticatory apocrypha (*Chenwei shu* 讖緯書), the many titles of which, with oracles and diagrams (*chenyu, tuchen*), are explicitly concerned with the semiology of dynastic transition.[69] A contemporary scholar's summation of the genre's significance for both national politics and its contribution to the formation of part of Daoist canon deserves a full qotuation:

> Undergirding the production of *chenwei* was a belief that Heaven signals its mandate for political change (and its ap-

proval of current policies) by sending not—any longer—just any sort of anomalies but a more specific type: strange texts, charts, talismans, and diagrams, in other words, unusual writings that are revealed spontaneously to humanity. As the roughly contemporaneous *Taipingjing* [Classic of Great Peace] succinctly put it, "When a great man is about to flourish, strange texts will appear" (*qiwen chu* 奇文出). That scripture, in fact, reveals a central concern with—as well as a detailed social program for—the collection of such "strange texts" and reports of other portents from all corners of the realm. It recommends the establishment of a roadside collection system for reports of portents and all other phenomena revelatory of the "intention of Heaven" (*tianyi* 天意) and the minds of the people, for, once assembled, these will in fact constitute revealed Daoist scriptures, the *Taipingjing* itself being a sort of meta-scripture detailing the way in which scriptures are to be received; it emphasizes the importance of circulating written documents as the medium for these reports; and it criticizes those of the Confucian eremetic tradition who shirk this grave social-moral-cosmic responsibility.[70]

The contest for political legitimacy thus turns on the proper reception and deployment of certain kinds of writing regarded as both revelation and talisman. The repeated use of the story of Li Hong directly anticipates the impact of Daoist prophecies during the early years of the Sui-Tang era in forecasting that the empire would finally belong to a clan with the name of Li.[71]

The widespread enlistment of nominal auguries, in both reigning monarchs and restive rebels, points once more to the importance of kinship terms in the dynamics of traditional Chinese politics. The teachings of religious Daoism might have placed the significance of the individual in a different light, since soteriological concerns must now be attended to and resolved with respect to the individual body. Even within such a discursive framework, the role of the ancestors, though changed, continues to command attention, because the individual adept's status and ritual action, according to an early scripture like the *Taipingjing*, may also decisively affect ancestral guilt and merit. Moreover, the religious focus on either antecedent life or eschatalogical bliss in no way alters the essence of political desire—that is, to become the supreme sovereign of the land, the name and status of which are also defined by the successful contender for the throne as the *founder* of a dynastic household. Lineage as a structural component of imperial governance thus maintains its uncontested valorization in both prospect and retrospect. Not surprisingly, therefore, one final device in legitimating such an aspiration to ultimate power, in Daoist rhetoric, is to unite ancestry with transcendent status and revelation. Emperor Zhenzong 真宗 (997–1022) of the Song, for example, would claim that his own ancestor was in fact a re-incarnated deity from the Daoist pantheon.[72]

Despite intermittent and fierce opposition by rival Confucians and Buddhists in the court, the beguiling knowledge promised by the other "country" of the Daoists thus also found acknowledgement in repeated imperial patronage. Tang emperors not only appointed many practicing Daoists as officials, but they had also sought institutional changes of their government in certain eras based on their devotion to the religion. Not only did many of them order the regular performance of Daoist rituals (along with Buddhist ones in different reign periods), but Emperor Gaozong in 674, for example, also promulgated an edict to make *Laozi* part of the required curriculum for the civil service examination, while Emperor Xuanzong in 749 established by edict the Chongxuan guan as a school with "doctors (*boshi*)," teaching assistants, and students for specific instruction of Daoist doctrines and texts. Without the unmatched resources of imperial patronage in different dynastic periods, the voluminous Daoist Canon (5,485 *juan* in 512 cases in the Zhengtong [1426–1436] edition) could hardly have come into existence or down to us in the form as we have it today. The history of its formation is a subject that merits a book-length treatment, but for our purpose here, we should note explicit imperial sponsorship and the provision of material assistance for the compilation, transcription, and (in later dynasties) the printing of the expanding Canon. The different rulers involved include Emperor Xuanzong in the Kaiyuan period (713–41); Taizong (976–97), Zhenzong (1008–1017), (1019), and Huizong (1102–1107) of the Northern Song; Xiaozong (1174–90) of the Southern Song; Taizong of the Yuan (1237–44); and Yingzong (1444–48), Shizong (1522–67), and Shenzong (1573–1620) of the Ming.

5

Buddhism:
The Challenge of Another Culture

ALTHOUGH THE TIME OF BUDDHISM'S FIRST ARRIVAL in China cannot be traced to a precise date, there is scholarly consensus that the spread of the faith could have reached China in as early a period as that between the last half century B.C.E. to the first half of the first century C.E.[1]

Like Confucianism and Daoism, its chief rival faiths native to China, Buddhism from its inception as a religion has been vitally linked with the ruling classes, first in India, the land of its origin, and frequently in the territories of its evangelization as it spread eastward. Its putative founder, Gautama Siddhārtha (ca. 566–486 B.C.E.), was himself a prince of a tiny kingdom, born in Kapilavastu, a place located in northeast India at what is now southern Nepal. Despite his rearing in palatial life and its presumed luxury, the prince found no peace or satisfaction with his existence, haunted by a keen awareness of pervasive suffering in the sentient world. His determined search for enlightenment came only after having gone through protracted periods of experimentation with different forms of asceticism, from the strictest disciplines to the more balanced style called the Middle Path. In the end, according to the tale familiar to all Buddhists, the prince sat down beneath a tree named the Bodhi Tree and decided never to raise himself again until he found his answer to suffering and death. When he finally broke through from ignorance to transforming knowledge, his altered understanding, in Buddhist discourse, is often likened to an awakening (from sleep or drunkenness) or attaining a different kind of consciousness (most commonly rendered in Chinese as *jue* 覺

and *wu* 悟). The prince is thereby named a Buddha, meaning the enlightened one (*futu* 浮屠, *fo* 佛).

Rising from the tree that enabled his meditation and enlightenment, Gautama, according to the Buddhist tradition, taught for four decades as an itinerant teacher throughout India, making numerous converts as his disciples. After his death, the disciples continued the evangelistic mission, and the teachings now assuming the form of a faith tradition rapidly expanded both numerically and geograhically. Roughly two centuries after the Buddha came another most famous Buddhist ruler in the person of the Indian monarch Aśoka, whose reign was *ca.* 272–236 B.C.E. According to Buddhist legend, he converted to Buddhism after having participated in bloody campaigns for years, and his newfound zeal led him to become one of the religion's most effective and cherished elite champions. In sum, he promoted the Buddhist *Dharma* to become the law of his kingdom, appointed ministers accordingly to promulgate such law to his subjects, advocated tolerance and common ethical observances, actively sponsored both religious rituals and the construction of sacred edifices (one legend claims that he built 84,000 stupas or reliquary mounds in his lifetime), and—most important for the expansion of the religion— supported and dispatched missionaries to propagate the faith beyond his native land. That last endeavor apparently made such a lasting impression on the entire Buddhist community that even six or seven hundred years after his time, Buddhist apologists in China would still argue that their own nation was a direct beneficiary of Aśoka's evangelistic policies, even though the earliest Chinese converts had been probably the progeny of contacts with Central Asian and Iranian traders and Parthian monks. The model of kingship that he espoused and personified, as we shall see presently, exerted also lasting impact on Chinese politics and imperial life.

As a context for that topic to be taken up in our present study, some further word, however brief, must be attempted to account for Buddhism's general impact on Chinese civilization. Since the dawn of Chinese modernity (whether dated as coincidental with the Ming or later with the decline of the Qing in the nineteenth century), scholars have been debating whether Buddhism had "conquered" China or whether Chinese culture, in turn, had "transformed" and thereby sinicized this Indian religion.[2] To say that there may be some truth to both assertions may be a preferred option for many students of Chinese Buddhism intent on avoiding oversimplification or needless conflict, but it may also obscure the fact that despite two millennia of the religion's accommodated existence in China, that existence in any Chinese society—in the past or at present, in Chinese territory or in diaspora—can be fraught with tension. The tension, we should try to remember, has been generated by the magnitude and scope of both Buddhism and its embedded culture's impact on the land and people it sought to convert. The practices and doctrines of the religion may be so at odds with native assumptions and values that, whether openly acknowledged or not, continuous negotiations are required of its followers within a specifically Chinese context.

For almost the first thousand years of Buddhism's history in China, the tradition itself has been sustained, in great part, by both mercantile and religious traffic with India and Central Asia.[3] The stupendous success of Buddhism's advancement in the land—in terms of changes wrought in Chinese social, political, economic, and ecclesiastical life, iconographic and architectural arts, literature and linguistics, technological and scientific knowledge ranging from textile production and agriculture to metallurgy and medicine—came about as a result of a sustained exchange of cultures. The intercourse between China and India historically thus represented the most momentous and consequential meeting of two already highly developed civilizations, each possessive of immense cultural sophistication and achievement. At the time when Buddhism entered China, the latter nation had already had a literate and bookish culture for over a thousand years, but Indian Buddhism brought with it a language and a new world of writings that, in sheer scope and volume, both elicited tremendous response from the Chinese and produced profound alterations in the receiving culture.

In early twentieth century, the famous scholar, philosopher, and diplomat Hu Shi(h) had opined that Indian literary forms and inventiveness directly and decisively influenced Chinese culture in the development of imaginative fiction, in contrast to ancient Chinese fictive writings that began as anecdotal legends and episodic variants of historiographic prose.[4] Major themes and topics such as the "the rabbit in the moon (*yuetu* 月兔)," the use of the watermark on a boat to weigh an elephant, the belief in the dragon (*naga*) as the parent of the horse, and such mythic phrases as sweet dew (*ganlu* 甘露) and deathless liquid (*busi shui* 不死水) that Chinese frequently take for granted as native ideas are, according to knowledgeable research by scholars in China and elsewhere, actually imported materials from India. In that regard, Sanskrit as the most authoritative, classical literary language of India has had such a profound and far-reaching impact on China that its full effect has yet to be adequately studied and measured. In terms of formal features, Sanskrit is probably the most different from Chinese, because the Indian language is characterized by extremely complex grammar and morphology, whereas Chinese, a largely monosyllabic and non-morphological language, is virtually its diametrical opposite.

When the two mighty linguistic systems collided, astonishing results occurred. Long before China's contacts with the tongues and scripts of Europe and America, the encounter with Indian writing and speech produced an undertaking in translation (of both Sanskrit and Prakrit, the medieval vernacular) such that, in sheer volume, scope, and magnitude, the civilized world had never seen hitherto or repeated since. Apart from the thousands of titles that form the body of Buddhist scriptures, the Chinese canon also contains important volumes on lexicography, the science of translation, grammar, and linguistics that lamentably too few Chinese scholars have studied. It was estimated by Liang Qichao 梁啟超, the reformer and modern scholar, that Indian languages, directly or indirectly, had helped to enlarge Chinese vocabulary by at least 35,000 words, surpassing the thirty-some-odd thousand that Shakespeare bequeathed to the English language.[5] The impact of Sanskrit on Chinese culture, moreover, extends beyond translation and diction, for the recent investigations by Professors Rao Zongyi (Hong Kong), Tsu-lin Mei (Cornell), and Victor Mair (University of Pennsylvania) have demonstrated conclusively that tonal metrics (*shenglü* 聲律), the exceedingly complicated scheme of prosody built on the juxtaposition of different tones (perhaps better termed as pitches) that governs forms of pre-modern Chinese poetry such as regulated verse (*lüshi* 律詩), lyric (*ci* 詞), and song (*qu* 曲), all derived from the earnest attempt of the Chinese to imitate certain phonetic properties of the Sanskrit language. Those immortal lines of Li Bai, Du Fu, Bai Juyi, and Su Shi—and one could name any famous or obscure poet between the fifth and twentieth century whom the Chinese people cherish—could not have been written in the metrical forms that have come to be loved for all time without the direct stimulus of certain foreign linguistic features. Nor could the development of the modern Chinese vernacular as a *koine* or common language, a *putonghua*, have come about without a big push from the Buddhist religion.[6] Beyond prosody and speech, literary style was also affected by the distinctively Indian tendency to interweave prose narration with poetry, and this prosimetric feature was eventually and firmly enshrined in both elitist fiction and popular story-telling of a religious or secular nature.

If this brief account seems too monothematically concerned with matters of language, I should point out that Indian influence on Chinese historical culture extends far beyond language. Many spices and varieties of food, including such ordinary items as black and white pepper and carrots or more exotic items like ghee-butter, cheeses, and kumiss, were introduced to China from "the West," meaning in early medieval time the regions of India and Central Asia. Indian culture contributed to Chinese development of many facets of technology, encompassing some techniques of surgery, the medical use of certain analgesic or anesthetic substances, and the enlargement of herbal pharmaceutics. The importation of new forms of dance, music, and instruments, an all-too-familiar topic in Chinese literary history, directly helped to generate an entirely new poetic form, the lyric or *ci*, in the seventh and eighth centuries. Without Indian Buddhist contribution, oral and performative literatures no less than certain forms of visual arts (the transformational tableaux known as *bianxiang* 變相) would not have developed.[7] Evangelistic efforts of Buddhist communities sped up dramatically in the Tang dynasty the use of paper and printing as well, just as monastic education, according to contemporary scholarship, significantly modified even certain aspects of the imperial educational system.[8] In his *History of Chinese Vernacular Literature*, Hu Shi has argued for the inventiveness of the Indian imagination by citing the vivid descriptions of the Buddhist hell in both scriptures and preaching and the likely impact they had to have on the religious congregation. What we now know of Buddhist education and ritual would supplement Hu's basic insight, for the emphasis of the Saṅgha on effective oratory, public lecture, and the pervasive use of the vernacular all point towards a deepening awareness of rhetoric, of the power and technique of verbal persuasion in the oral, written, and visual media. It is thus not surprising that the recorded sayings of Zen Masters (*Chan yulu*) and their method of dialogical instruction were readily adopted by Song Neo-Confucian thinkers and educators.

Such a massive transference and implantation of culture by themselves would have generated momentous reaction, if not necessarily determined resistance. What did elicit resistance and, at least in one area, potentially perpetual friction between the religion and the land of its evangelization was the new form of community envisaged by Buddhism. When Gautama began to expound his teachings after he found enlightenment, his preaching that produced disciples brought into existence a new form of community eventually named the Saṅgha, which traditionally was constituted by four groups of person—laymen, laywomen, monks, and nuns. Inserted into the social body of traditional China, this new community betokens an anomalous and incongruous growth—a source of incipient or open conflict with the culture because the factors of its formation and maintenance were so at odds with the long cherished assumptions held by the Chinese on human society. Although the history of that conflict is familiar to most students of Chinese Buddhism, it bears brief rehearsal here because it can help to reveal once again the religion's inevitable entanglement with state politics.

Prior to the influx of Buddhism to China, the fundamental unity posited between the realms of ethics and politics was based on the affirmed continuity between clan and court, between family and state. The Confucian homology of virtue, crystallized in the concept of filial piety, means that a single "way" of attitude and conduct is normatively applicable in both the personal (what we now call private) and the public (the impersonally political) spheres. "When we take that by which we serve the father to serve the mother," declares the *Classic of Filial Piety* (*Xiaojing* 孝經), "the love is the same. When we take that by which we serve the father to serve the ruler, the reverence is the same. Thus the mother takes one's love, whereas the ruler takes one's reverence. He who who takes both is the father. Therefore, when one uses filial piety to serve one's ruler, one will be loyal 故以孝事君則忠."[9] The conclusion is strengthened by the further supposition that a filial person also observant of fraternal reverence (*xiaodi* 孝弟) would be disinclined to affront his superiors and incite rebellions (*Analects* 1.2). Although various schools of thinking in classical China had sought to diminish the power and vice of the princes through criticism, none of them had ever thought of re-envisioning the bond of society in anything other than kinship terms. Even religious Daoism, which placed considerable emphasis on the necessity of individual quest of salvation and its Northern Division (*beizong* 北宗) of which also advocated priestly celibacy, still functioned largely within the values of traditional society and its presumed structure of constitutive hierarchy. The Buddhist Saṅgha, on the other hand, represented a radical re-definition of human community as religious community by eliminating the biological factor, and with it, any valorization of kinship ties. The religious community exists then and now not only as a separate community, but its very separateness, induced and supported by the believers' departure from the home and by the doctrine of clerical celibacy, requires the de-emphasis, if not its total repudiation, of the basis of society as the Han Chinese seemed to have always imagined and advocated it. The promoted separateness, in turn, has meant the weakening of the crucial actions and structures supportive of Chinese society.

Chinese reaction to Buddhism and their critique of the religion thus understandably center on what is perceived as a frontal assault on the family and household, and the criticism in the wake of the religion's diffused expansion in the culture focuses on the matter of the believer's altered relations with one's parents. In the trenchant words of the following quotation,

> The teaching/religion of Confucius of the Zhou regards filial piety as the paragon; when filiality is held as the ultimate of virtues, it is the root of a hundred actions. When the root is established, the Way comes to birth and reaches up to even the divine luminaries. Thus the way that a son serves his parents would assume the care of their feeding while they are alive, and when they die, he would honor them with their ritual sacrifices. Filial obligations may number to three thousand strong, but none is greater than providing a male for posterity. Since one's body comes from one's father and mother, one dares not in any way harm or injure it. . . . The way of Śramaṇa, on the other hand, would destroy and leave those who have given us life, for abandoning one's parents means we become distant to them. . . . The kin of flesh and bones are regarded as strangers on the road. There is nothing greater than such transgression of principles and injury of human feelings. Nonetheless, it still insists on enlarging the Way and enhancing benevolence so as to succor widely the multitudes. In point of fact, how could such action differ from digging up the roots and using them as a means to prune the branches? . . . . When even skins are discarded, to what could feather and fur be attached?[10]

This expansive piece of recorded criticism by an official of the Jin (265–419) during the first phase of intensive Buddhist-Confucian polemical conflict touches on many of the salient faults that the Chinese would find with the teachings of Buddhism with respect to the home and family life. To leave one's home represents veritable acts of criminality that include abandoning one's parents to join the Saṅgha or lead a life of mendicancy, the cessation of ancestral sacrifices, the mutilation of one's body (by shaving one's hair when one becomes a nun or priest), and the effective severance of one's lineage by taking the vow of celibacy if the family has no other male heir alive.

Honoring one's parents, as developed in the Confucian discourse, involves, of course, more than merely food for their living and sacrifices when they embark on their post-mortem way to becoming honored ancestors. The heart of the matter lies also in the heart; hence the famous observation by Confucius: "One knows even how to feed one's dogs and horses. Without reverence, what's the difference!" (*Analects* 2. 7). Because the clerics are forbidden to bow or kneel to lay persons, their refusal to kowtow to their kin after ordination has always tended to offend the historical Chinese populace of high or low ranks alike. As a critic has observed: "When the son first leaves home [to take up the priestly vocation], and when the mother follows as a nun, she would be required to honor first her own son. This is a gross transgression of proper propriety!"[11]

Religious celibacy violates not only the mandatory obligation of lineage maintenance, but it also disrupts radically the institution of marriage, named in the Confucian discourse as "a great relations of the human 人之大倫." As a courageous official, Xun Ji 荀濟 of the Liang (as recorded in a treatise by the seventh-century Tang priest, Daoxuan), declares in his critical memorial to the ardent Buddhist emperor Wudi: "Nowadays monks and nuns would not plow the fields nor marry, and they thus completely abrogated reproduction . . . . This is their first offense against canonical morality. . . . All of us living sentients unite as husbands and wives in order to bear sons and daughters, but the laws of the barbarians (*hufa* 胡法) reverse the matter. . . . This is their second offense against canonical morality. . . . They practice abortion to kill their sons, and yet they would feed mosquitoes and their eggs [because this is the way Buddhists obey the injunction not to take life?]."[12] The charge of abrogating the normative duty of reproduction, under the suasion of an alien religion no less, understandably also extends to the denunciation of the believers' neglect of caring for the livelihood of parents, wives, and children. This latter accusation actually stems from the objection to the Buddhist practice of charity donations beyond clan and home, and the alleged detriment to one's household thus represents another affront to the Confucian ethical code of first assisting one's own kin.[13]

As we know from the history of early Chinese Buddhism, all such objections received polemical rebuttal from learned priests and lay officials with varying success.[14] On the issue of filial piety, the tact repeatedly taken by the Buddhist defense is to emphasize the spiritual benefits that parents can derive from the child's piety. The son's decision to leave the home in religious devotion (*chujia* 出家 or *pravaj*), though it may seem a momentary denial of parental care in this life, would actually work for incalculable benefits for the parental salvation in the next world. As in the promise of Daoism, the Buddhist religion magnifies dramatically the importance of the hereafter in the Chinese consciousness. Eschatological merit conferred by the son thereby reverses ritual obligations prescribed for the present existence. Hence the tremendous appeal of the story of Mulian or Maudgalyāyana, whose pious devotion also provided him with sufficient magic power to rescue eventually his sinful mother from the horrid sufferings in the Avīci hell. Different scriptural interpretations began to render Gautama himself a more filial son; by the time of the Tang, an erudite priest like Zongmi 宗密 (780–841), in his commentary on the *Yulan pen jing* 盂蘭盆經, would attempt to bring Confucianism and Buddhism closer by accentuating systematically the regard for filial piety by exemplary Buddhist figures and the spiritual benefits accrued to parents on account of their children's religious virtues.[15]

As for the treatment of ancestors, we have records showing that priests and nuns did begin to participate in memorial services for imperial ancestors and deceased emperors within their monasteries during the time of the Tang, and the imperial court also encouraged clerical participation in such rituals. Concerning their own familial forbearers, the Buddhist teaching of the intermediate stages of the deceased soul's transmigration (seven days for one stage, and the soul must experience seven such stages before attaining the proper next rebirth) and the crucial need for someone living to produce ritual merit on behalf of the deceased—a doctrine possibly deriving from the Hindu rites of ancestor making mentioned earlier in this study—thus complicates the Chinese concern for the dead while enlarging at the same time the contribution of the clergy. Even in modern Buddhism, the ritual period of forty-nine days of grand mass for the dead continues this traditional emphasis.

Apart from the all-important matter of ancestor worship, further efforts in modifying Buddhist doctrines and practices to mollify Chinese sentiments took the form of harmonizing ethical teachings. As early as the Northern Wei, there was the proposal of using the Five Śīlas (*wujie* 五戒) of not killing, stealing, committing adultery, telling lies, and drinking liquor to parallel the Confucian norms of benevolence, justice, propriety, knowledge, and trustworthiness (*ren, yi, li, zhi, xin*). In later imperial periods, greater allowance was made for laypersons to practice the faith within the confines of the family compound, and devotional studios, quiet rooms, and shrines would be consecrated either in the home or somewhere in the courtyard.

Acculturation on the part of the incoming religion and accommodation on the part of the native culture, however,

did not mean the assured cessation of conflict or the pre-
vention of new tension from arising in the society. During
the intellectually turbulent centuries of the Northern Song
when the combined efforts of certain leading elite officials
and thinkers sought to revitalize Confucianism by clarify-
ing and reconceptualizing its cardinal tenets to meet the
Buddhist challenge, available textual materials under the
most current examination tend to indicate how Buddhism
itself—at least among some of its own prominent clerics
and sympathizers—was directly or indirectly instrumental
in assisting the renaissance of its rival religion or ideology,
leading thus to the re-affirmation of the Confucian rel-
evance and contribution towards securing the a legitimate
form of order in a human society.[16] That kind of acknowledgement and even theoretical concession, however, does
not eliminate fresh bones of contention and contestation.
Enlistment of Buddhist clergy in mourning and burial rites,
mentioned just previously, led quickly to Confucian misgiv-
ings and renewed critique. Against the very ritual of funeral
service lasting till the "seventh seventh day," the Song
historian and official Sima Guang 司馬光 (1019–1086) had
some harsh words against "the deceit and deceptions of
the Buddhists." Convinced that "with death the physical
form and the spirit separate, in such a way that the body
entering the yellow earth would rot and deterioate as wood
and stone, and that the spirit would drift like wind and fire
to who knows where," Sima refused to validate the sufferings inflicted by the Buddhist hells widely disseminated in
popular preaching and cautionary Buddhist tales. He also
quoted with approval a saying attributed to the Tang mag-
istrate Li Dan 李丹 that the belief in the possibility of one's
parents receiving punishment in hell would betray a wholly
unacceptable assumption that those parents were "people
laden with wickedness and sins 積惡有罪之人."[17] Renewed
hostility to the diffused and pervasive Buddhist presence

in Song China was not fueled merely by the utility of burial rites. Since her early arrival in China with the inception of Buddhism, the unrivalled ascendence of the Bodhisattva Avalokiteśvara or Guanyin through a protracted process of transformation in the country's various regions and cultic centers to become the most popular Chinese goddess most sensitive and reponsive to female religiosity within a society of entrenched and unapologetic patriarchalism already indicated one cardinal reason for both the irresistible appeal of the religion to this day and its challenge to certain cherished norms of value and behavior.[18] The attraction of the religion for women elite and demotic alike consists in the several kinds of provision proffered by the faith. Socially and culturally, there were the emphasis on the special compassion of the Boddhisattva Guanyin, and the proliferation of "the books of good works [shanshu 善書]" and "precious scrolls [baojuan 寶卷]" as devotional literature that cater, even if not exclusively, to a women readership.[19] Various social services undertaken by lay religious associations specifically concerned with the care of women also emerged during the latter part of imperial society. Doctrinally and emotionally, Buddhism thus offers women comfort, companionship, and assurance of worth in this life no less than the hope for eschatological betterment in the next world—that, despite the unresolved problem of whether a female, in formal Buddhist dogma, can attain Buddhahood.[20] Communally, the Saṅgha that is housed separately in temples, shrines, abbeys, monastic halls or retreat edifices proffers a socio-religious space for conversation, fellowship, and ritual sustenance. All such ideological and programmatic endeavors, however, understandably also aroused the wholesale resistance and denunciation from Confucian male elites from the time of the Song onward. In this light, even someone like Zhu Xi himself could hardly be expected to be free from some of the longstanding objections raised against rivalling religions deemed detrimental to Confucian values. His experience of officialdom made it obvious to him that some of the ritual ideals and practices, such as encouraging women to lead a reclusive and even celibate life away from home to practice cultivation or religious austeries, were freely passed on from Buddhism to the Daoist communities.[21] Unrestrained pursuit of such religious ideals, as the polemical charge was levied against the Buddhist tradition, would lead to the unimaginable disaster of terminating human progeny itself. According to the introductory remarks of another recent study,

> Dispensing praise and blame in descriptive, prescriptive, and fictional writings, the [later Ming-Qing] Confucian polemicists undertook to re-sacralize women's domestic role, denounce the temple-centered religious activities, and defend the ancestral altar as the holy place par excellence. . . . Writers with diverse sympathies, motives, and audiences reveal the central concerns and shared bottom line of the discourse. That is, women's extra-domestic religious activities threaten the foundation and fabric of the Confucian family order; spatial control is the key to the control of the stringently defined female religiosity and the relaxation of one spells the collapse of the other.[22]

The Confucian family order, of course, is both a fundamental and a reciprocal paradigm for the order of the imperial state as imagined and sustained by the Confucian state cult discourse. This sketch of the Buddhist religion's interaction with traditional Chinese society and culture thus perforce must return to the central topic of politics itself, though our discussion thereof will also touch on only the most pertinent points of interest. History has intimated that Buddhist contact with Chinese rulers was practically coterminous with its entrance into the land itself. Apart from the more fantastic tales of different dreams of emperors depicting either imagistically or symbolically the arrival of Buddhism, there was the early textual allusion (in 65 C.E.) from an imperial edict to Prince Ying of Chu who, "for his special fondness for Huang-Lao learning in his latter years, was keeping ritual diets and making sacrifices to Buddha, . . . [including] the preparation of lavish feasts for fasting (*Upavāsa*) ascetics (*Śramaṇa*)."[23] If this little report had any factual basis, it would mean not only that sizeable Buddhist communities were already established and in fairly intimate contact with the upper strata of Eastern Han society at that time, but also that, as a modern scholar had observed, some common Buddhist terms in Sanskrit transcribed through Chinese phonemes made their sudden but unobtrusive appearance in an official document.[24] Although for the next two plus centuries, as Liang Qichao noted further, there was no widespread discussion among many of the literate elites, whether holding office or not, that indicated what might have been their reaction to the escalating presence of Buddhist communities and ideas, the religion's impact on court life and policies was another matter.[25] The potential clash with Chinese imperial self-identity and self-understanding was inevitable, because one of the most exalted discourses ever fashioned for characterizing a human sovereign was suddenly confronted with another tradition of ritual, speech, and manner that seemed completely impudent, if not downright lawless!

"Not only did the Buddhist monks feel that they were under no obligation to pay homage to the ruler," as Kenneth Ch'en had pointed out succinctly, "but it also appears that they regarded kings in an unfavorable light, as unworthy of reverence" on account of their unflattering and blunt assessment of royal covetousness and lust for power.[26] Understandably, this conviction of the essential independence of the Saṅgha, not subject to other forms of ethical or political authority but to its own internal laws and regulations, was branded repeatedly as a total violation of the peculiar and totalizing claim of the imperial institution, for as a Buddhist specialist has long observed,

> Chinese society regarded itself not merely as one nation inhabiting one plot of earth and living by one set of manners. It regarded itself as the only civilized society on earth, the only one living by a set of rules that matched the Macrocosmic Order. The destiny of all mankind, according to this view, was to become "Chinese", in the sense not of acquiring a juridical change of nationhood but of accepting the only civilized way of life in existence. The Chinese Emperor, according to the same view, was not merely a chief of state among chiefs of state, nor even a *primus inter pares*, but the Vicar of Heaven on Earth, the rightful source of all temporal authority. If certain persons failed to recognize that authority, it was through ignorance or out of malice, but it was never justifiable. Consequently the Chinese traditionalist could recognize no class of beings that is in the world but not of it. For such a person the Buddhist monk on Chinese soil was an intolerable anomaly.[27]

For the five centuries ranging from the mid-third century c.e. down to the eighth century, from the early time of China's Disunion Period to the eventual reunification of the High Tang, the fortunes of the Buddhist tradition were thus of necessity intimately intertwined with the vicissitudes of politics by polemically defending its peculiar socio-political ideals, garnering imperial patronage and support amidst sporadically intense rivalry and conflict with court Daoism and Confucianism, accommodating the steadily expanding efforts of the court to regulate and control the vital activities of the Saṅgha in exchange for certain benefits such as tax and military conscription exemption (no small or easy privilege for the young males in view of Chinese law, ancient and modern), seeking outright donation of land from royal or gentry households, and, in the process, weathering at least three violent outbursts of imperial persecutions.

Despite the gyrating fortunes of the period and occasional setbacks, Buddhism as a whole not merely survived its initial success in pervasive entrance into all parts of Chinese society but also went on to flourish during the Tang into the Song to become an ineradicable part of Chinese religious life.[28]

In terms of the treacherous issue of homage to the sovereign ruler, the controversy precipitated attacks from powerful officials upholding the ritual of emperor veneration and counter-arguments advanced by a learned cleric like Huiyuan 慧遠 (334–416). The immediate provocation of the monk's polemics was occasioned by one Huan Xuan 桓玄, who sought to usurp the throne of the Jin by setting up in 399 an indepent satrap in south China. Though familiar with both Daoist and Buddhist doctrines as a highly literate person, Huan's military background also made him suspicious of the clerical presence and involvement in court. The specific legislations he proposed for his own state thus also sought to purge the Saṅgha of tax and labor evasion and to insist on clerical homage for the ruler. Huan's letter of 402 to his six departmental heads and two officers of his Palace Secretariat appeals to Laozi's declaration (in *Daodejing* 25) that the king (*wang*) shares the epithet of "great (*da*)" with the other three emblems of greatness—namely, Dao, Heaven, and Earth. The Daoist emphasis here, according to Huan's next allusion to *Zhuangzi* 2 and 14, is on the matter of "fecundating life and interchanging fated rotation (*zisheng tongyun* 資生通運)." The power of the ruler thus adduced from the two Daoist documents leads Huan to conclude that : "the great virtue of Heaven and Earth is said to be life, but [the power] of interchanging life and putting things in order resides in the kingly one 天地之大德曰生，通生理物存乎王者." [29] Hence no human cleric is exempt from the sovereign's life-giving and -changing power.

In the lengthy history of the Chinese discourse intent

on promoting imperial status and potency, Huan's self-aggrandizing pronouncement of his godlike authority is hardly novel. According to Zhang Rongming, this discourse that sought to divinize the ruler (*shensheng di tongzhizhe* 神聖的統治者) runs the gamut of documents in the ancient and classical periods. The recurrent exaltation of the ruler in the political, moral, and ritual texts unfolds at least in four inter-related formulations: that the king is the true progeny of the High God/Ancestor (上帝的嫡子), that the emperor as "the true dragon Son of Heaven (真龙天子)" is the one who "obeys Heaven and bears [in his person] the fated rotation (奉天承運)," that the imperial government is a de facto "instrumentalized priestly organization (工具化的祭司机构)," and that the "overlord (君主)" is, as we have pointed out in Chapter 1 of the present study, the person responsible for auspicious or disastrous omens of the domain. Relative to each of these theses have developed further elaborations of imperial status and power. To substantiate the thesis about the "true dragon Son of Heaven," for example, Zhang enumerates such descriptions of the emperor as "a type of [unusual] pneumatic endowment (秉气型)," "a type of extraordinary anatomy (生理超凡型)," "a progeny of oneiric portent (托梦型)," "a progeny of dragon impregnation (龙子型)," "a type of theanthropos (神人型)," "a type of the progeny of scarlet radiance (赤光型)," and "a type of an incarnate Buddha or Boddhisattva (托於佛门型)."[30]

This sustained exercise of rhetorical and ritual magnification of the emperor's significance as well as the meaning of the imperium for the Chinese social order, in turn, measures the audacity of Huiyuan's language and thought. The shocking brilliance of his famous treatise, "Shamen bujing wangzhe lun 沙門不敬王者論" (404), stems from its insertion into the dominant cultural discourse of China, with undisguised directness, the strange notion that life as biological existence is not necessarily a good and an end in itself, thereby abrogating at once also a human person's obligatory indebtedness to one's ancestors, parents, and, by crucial extension, one's ruler. Drawing extensively from the diction and rhetoric of early Daoist thinkers like Laozi and Zhuangzi, Huiyuan contends that for the priest

> who has left the household, life is a lodger beyond the clan boundaries (*fang* 方), his traces . . . cut off from those of the beings. The Doctrine/Religion (*jiao* 教) by which he lives enables him to understand that woes and impediments come from having a body, that by not maintaining the body one terminates woe. He knows that continuing life comes from undergoing transformation, but the matter of seeking the First Principle (*zong* 宗) cannot be based on submission to transformation (*shunhua* 順化, Buddhist metaphor for death). Because he seeks the First Principle not through submitting to transformation, [the priest] does not valorize the resource of rotational interchange (*yuntong zhi zi* 運通之資 [hence Buddhist wisdom surpasses even Daoist insight]).[31] If the termination of woe does not stem from the preservation of the body, then he does not value the virtues that enhance life (息患不由 於存身，則不貴厚生之德 [hence Buddhist wisdom is superior to Confucian tenet]).[32]

The grand, linear Confucian narrative woven from the interlocking concepts of life's origin, ancestor, sovereign, and patriarch and its derived mandates for ethics and politics is hereby ruptured, directly contradicted by the commitment of a human individual determined not to foster or enhance life, for life in this person's estimate is fundamentally beset by suffering.

Huiyuan defines a Buddhist cleric as someone "who turns against Origin in quest of the First Principle (反本求宗者)." In such a person's view, "although Heaven and Earth regard as Great the [matter of] keeping life alive, these two powers cannot cause the living beings not to undergo transformations [that is, to prevent them from dying]. [Similarly], kings and

dukes might consider the preservation of existence as meritorious achievement, but they cannot prevent those existing
from impediments and woes 天地雖以生生為大，而未能令
生者不化。王侯雖以存存為功，而未能令存者無患。"[33] On
this basis, one owes neither life nor its giver one's necessary gratitude, even though the priest's cultivated indiffer-
ence to parents and rulers, in the last analysis, is not to be
construed as insolence or impiety. In view of the pervasive
suffering in existence, sentient life for the Buddhist, inspired
especially by the exemplary figure of the compassionate
Bodhisattva, is that it may serve as a sacrificial gift for other
lives, an act of resolute altruism directed away from kin
and clan. It is not to be clung to as a cherished possession
reserved only for the requittal of parental and ancestral
largesse.[34] Such an argument, along with others made by
Buddhist apologists, did not win for the Buddhist Saṅgha a
status of permanent independence from state control and
regulation. What the public presentation of the argument
did reveal once more was how certain forms of religious life
in historical China could certainly be expected to come into
severe conflict with the cherished assumptions underlying
the dominant culture, assumptions that, as I have argued,
had also a religious basis. For Buddhism, according to
E. Zürcher's astute observation, "had to seek recognition in
a society where the conception of governmental (in theory,
imperial) authority was incompatible with the existence of
an asocial, improductive and autonomous body within the
state, and where systems of thought used to be evaluated
according to their practical efficacy rather than to their religous and metaphysical merits."[35] Moreover, what Huiyuan's
remark further discloses, as I shall argue in the closing part
of this chapter, is the advancement of a highly individu-
alistic mode of religious consciousness, one that radically
challenges the Chinese assumption of seamless continuity
of exemplar and resonance (and thus, too, of obligation and

response) between cosmic order, political sovereignty, and mundane existence.

According to familiar accounts in scholarship, the controversy over whether the monks should pay homage to the emperor lasted for nearly four centuries, and eventually the result reached the uneasy closure of a draw in the contest. The Tang emperor Gaozong's edict of 662 exempted clerics from ceremonious acts toward the emperor but insisted on prostration to parents as their due action of gratitude. Unlike Indian monarchs, however, Chinese emperors reciprocally were not expected to stand up or perform any action of reverence for the clergy of any religion either.[36] With the gradual cessation of this controversy, other issues concerning state regulation that occupied continuous attention and debate included priestly registration, limiting the numbers of clerics, and the control of investitures and their financial windfall for the imperial treasury. As Buddhist schools flourished and multiplied, the state's intervention in the matter of priestly ordination meant also its intrusion into the education and certification of the clergy through the regulation and modification of curriculum content and requirements, including even at times the discrimination of heresy. On the matter of clerical morals in relation to state laws, a basic code governing the conduct of Daoist and Buddhist clergy titled *Daoseng ge* 道僧格, a text no longer extant but that might have found preservation in the Japanese work *Sōni-ryō* 僧尼令, undertook the perplexing task of sorting out penalties for different offenses of the clergy that might have both religious and civil implications (for example, adultery, intoxication, or theft).[37] Co-optation of support from the Saṅgha gave rise to a protracted policy of appointing priests to bureaucratic posts and enlisting their participation in governmental programs, including the conducting and maintenance of religious services inside the palatial buildings proper for imperial patronage use. At time of military emergencies arising from rebellions or invasions, palatial clerics were commanded to recite sutras for the state's protection from all kinds of calamities ranging from natural evils to military defeats and foreign incursions. Such an arrangement explains the popularity of the *Scripture for Humane Kings* (*Renwang jing* 人王經), twice translated and well preserved in the canon.[38] And finally, the escalating bureaucratic control meant the proliferation of institutional agencies that had oversight of the Buddhist community and its activities. Beginning with the start of the Northern Wei at 356 C.E. down to the mid-Tang, a series of new official posts and governmental units were named to supervise religious activities of the realm. At the height of Buddhist eminence during the reign of Emperor Taizong of the Tang (627–50), the potent office of Commissioner of Meritorious Works (*gongde shi* 功德使) was created and its entrusted holder teemed with some of the most ardent and powerful Buddhist prime minsiters and officials of the period.

The above sketch of the Buddhist tradition's interaction with Chinese imperial politics, though dependent in many ways on Kenneth Ch'en's informative chapter on the topic, does not accept entirely his conclusion. He was of the firm opinion that "the sangha accepted and came to terms with the prevailing Confucian ideology of the supremacy of the state over any religious association within its borders,"[39] a thesis that now requires some modification in the light of more recent scholarship. The pioneering studies by Professor Gu Zhengmei 古正美, the magnitude and scope of which defies convenient summary in our present work, nonetheless requires a brief mention. Her compendious and meticulous account of the political fortunes and policies of numerous rulers (both Han and non-Han), starting from the Huandi 桓帝 period of the Han (147–68) down to the Qianlong 乾隆 (1735–95) of the Qing, provides irrefutable demonstration that Buddhist beliefs and values (what she terms "ideology") have for more than fifteen hundred years continued to shape and modify political consciousness of the ruling elites no less than the demotic masses. Although during the North-South disunion era, the majority of rulers governing Chinese territory were non-Han foreigners, there was no lack of Han emperors devoted to the enlistment of Buddhism for governance from the times of the Liang (502–557), the Sui (581–617), and the Tang.[40] It is to her credit, moreover, that her investigations serve to confirm the findings of other colleagues concerning politics and religion in pre-modern China: that (1) the imperial state is undergirded more by a religious than a secular ideology, that (2) the contentious debate and formulation of imperial policies under various dynastic regimes continue to reflect the contending forces of the Three Religions and their sympathizers, and that (3) the ritual norms and practices upheld by the state cult administrative and educational bureaucracies, though unambiguously Confucian, do not thereby eliminate effectively all dissenting voices even in the imperial court.

Most important of all, her magisterial research into the developmental history of King Aśoka's political idealism has clarified more than ever the careful planning and deliberate implementation of policies exercised by a "usurper" ruler like Wu Zetian (690–705) of the Tang in her drive to become the first woman Buddhist cakravartin.[41] Not only were both the politics and gender of Wu galling to Confucian loyalists at the time, but the very model of her political aspiration has also not been adequately understood even in modern Chinese scholarship until recently. An accepted authority as Xiao Gongquan could declare in his acclaimed *History of Chinese Politics*: "for Buddhism was originally a religion and not a form of political thought. Coincidentally, its pessimistic, other-worldly view of life also seems rather close to the thinking of Laozi and Zhuangzi. Thus it is to be expected that it can offer little contribution to political thought."[42]

Xiao's sweeping remark betrays virtually the total ignorance of the early history of Indian Buddhism and its profound impact on the development of Buddhist notions of sacral kingship that found lasting embodiment in King Aśoka, the illustrious monarch of the Kushāns dynasty (50–244 C.E.). In turn, the man's lifelong ambition to live and rule as the paradigmatic Buddhist king (the *Buddharāja* or *fowang* 佛王), itself most likely a derivative continuance of the Hindu motif of the Celestial King (the *Devarāja* or *Maheśvara* or *tianwang* 天王, a term the figural and iconographic embodiments of which, in fact, had been vastly appropriated eventually by popular religions in China), has exerted incalculable influence on the imperial rulers down through Chinese history.[43] Returning momentarily to the little story of Prince Ying of the first century, we should note that the account does not highlight merely the aging prince's religious predilection of "delight in the subtle words of Huang-Lao and holding ritual feasts and sacrifices for Buddha." As the story unfolds in the biography, the Prince was officially accused of "entertaining seditious plans 有逆謀," manufacturing "golden tortoises and jade cranes, and carving scripted words as forms of auspicious talisman 刻文字以為符瑞," and, most dangerously of all, "altering arbitrarily governmental rankings and installing various earls, princes, dukes, and generals commanding two thousand piculs of rice as their salaries." We do not know to which religious tradition those scripted words belong; as emergent Daoism was developing a different and separate theory of script and language already, the forms of these material symbols (tortoises and cranes apart from scripted words) might well represent an affinity with Daoism.[44] In view, however, of what had been noted in our previous section on Daoist exploitation of nominal or semiological auguries for political purposes, Gu Zhengmei's analysis of Prince Ying's action as likely implicated in "political activities for nation building" is highly plausible.[45] Because of Emperor Mingdi's "love for kin (*qinqin*)," Prince Ying was pardoned, and his feast for Buddhist clergy and sacrifices, in fact, were paid for as his "fines." Nonetheless, his eventual suicide not only terminated his single life but also involved the imprisonment, death, and exile of over a thousand of his followers.[46]

Professor Gu's particular point about the possibility of Aśokan ideals reaching Prince Ying (because both their dates were rough parallels) might seem a bit speculative,[47] but the powerful effects of escalated contacts of Buddhists with the highest echelons of ruling classes and the repeated and sustained efforts on the part of either the rulers or their ministers and counselors to enlist Buddhist law and ideals to shape state policies cannot be controverted. Without the material and human resources intermittently lent by the court and powerful bureaucracies, such massive public projects as translations and the building of Buddhist edifices of all varieties—from the late Han to the Tang—could not have taken place at all. If, as we have seen, the Han rulers were regularly eager to seek out from the Daoists the advice, suggestion, and recommended material goods for the alleged betterment of their bodily existence, their encounter with Buddhist teachings became unmistakable in an incident like the early memorial from the scholar Xiang Kai 襄楷 in 166 c.e.[48] For our purpose here, the words of Xiang submitted for Emperor Huandi's consideration are significant not only because they quote from the *Sūtra of Forty-Two Sections*, but also because they propose an extensive exhortation for the sovereign to heed the Buddhist doctrines on purity, emptiness, and diminishment of desire, based on the exemplary act of Buddha himself in resisting the seduction by beautiful and lascivious women. Despite the syncretic blend of Huang-Lao themes threading through

the memorial, the rhetoric also embodies significant differences from the emphases of Daoist concepts and rituals or
the aphoristic formulations deriving from Confucian efforts
at moral self-cultivation. The thrust of Buddhist political
ideology here makes itself felt in the appeal for personal
emulation of a concrete religious personality. This appeal,
as Gu' studies have shown, will find protracted acceptance
and response in different guises down through the imperial
centuries.

Consistent with the thesis and theme of this study, my
focus has been trained on the early Chinese state and its
political involvement with religion. It would be a distorted
picture, however, if the sole, accumulated impression left
of this undertaking dwells on how religion has been only a
field of continuous appropriation and exploitation by the
imperial state, or that the state itself, despite contentious
rivalries and doctrinal controversies among different religious traditions, remained essentially an authoritarian but
tolerant apparatus. Even for the emperors themselves, as
we have intimated, Daoism, Buddhism, and possibly scattered variants of popular religious acts and beliefs manifestly have provided different venues for meeting personal
predilections and needs, sometimes with obvious relations
to their obligatory political concerns and sometimes not.
Whatever their personal inclinations or predilections, the
emperors themselves also were nothing if not wilful and
capricious beings. Though many of them might have been
kindly disposed towards Buddhism at one time or another,
they also proved themselves to be frequently changeable,
especially under the suasion of contending parties. Benevolent patronage in one season could swiftly alter to become
violent reprisal in another time of the same reign period. At
the end of this section of my study, I want to round out the
picture further by referring briefly to two different pictures
of imperial engagement with the Buddhist religion. One

concerns the familiar episodes of "The Destruction of the Dharma by the Three Wus 三武滅法," the circumstances of how three different emperors persecuted the Saṅgha in different periods. The other takes up the story of what may be the most famous Buddhist personality of Chinese history to illustrate another dimension of our consideration: namely, that religion historically could and did serve as a potent enablement against the monolithic power of the state. That personality is Chen Xuanzang 陳玄奘 (596–664), the most famous and celebrated scripture-pilgrim of the entire tradition.

The first case of major persecution arose in the reign of Taiwudi 太武帝 (r. 424–52) of the Tuoba Wei dynasty (386–532). Despite the widespread acceptance of Buddhism among the Tuoba 拓跋 (literally, "born to the sheets") people, and the favorable patronage of the tradition by the first two empeors, Daowu and Mingyuan, the third emperor became much more enamored with Daoism, but his change of attitude, ironically, was brought about by the schemes of an ambitious minister, Cui Hao 崔浩 (381–450), who was also an ardent Confucian in collaboration with a Daoist reformer. Apparently, Cui's tortuous personal history in politics—alternately falling in and out of imperial favor—also implicated Kou Qianzhi. The latter was himself not without towering ambition, seeking, in fact, to rejuvenate at this time the Celestial Master tradition and turn this form of Daoism into the state religion of the Northern Wei, possibly with himself as "Pope" of the community. Kou was both befriended and exploited by Cui, and the target of their self-aggrandizing policy was the Buddhist Saṅgha. In 426 when emperor Taiwu wanted to attack the inhabitants in northwest Guanzhong, his own military commander hesistated for fear of the enemy's military strength. Kou, however, encouraged the throne with the assurance that the emperor's "divine prowess would make a timely manifestation, as Heaven's guidance [would result in] order down below. Therefore, he should use his troops to pacify all Nine Provinces [the whole of known China], deploying arms first and civil governance thereafter, so that he can become the Perfected Lord of Supreme Peace (Taiping Zhenjun 太平真君)." From that time till late in 439, the emperor indeed enjoyed several highly successful campaigns and crushed all resistance. To unify his rule in the entire northern region, he changed the name of his reign period to Taiping in 440 and also assumed the title proposed by Cui.

The action against the Buddhists, however, began in 438 with an imperial edict proscribing anyone under fifty joining the Saṅgha. Because three thousand monks were among those resisting the Wei's forces against Liangzhou in 439 and then taken as prisoners, the emperor would have executed all of them had not Kou interceded and had them placed instead in labor camps. In 445, another rebellion broke out among the ethnic residents of Guanzhong led by one Gai Wu 蓋吳. After the government troops sent to suppress them broke into the monastery grounds of Chang'an, they discovered horses and such a huge cache of weapons as bows, arrows, shields, and spears. Inside the temples were also "underground rooms appointed for debauchery with women of aristocratic families." In fury, Taiwu accepted Cui Hao's recommendation and decreed that all monks of Chang'an be executed. Another edict of 446 not only ordered that temples of the whole country be destroyed and the scriptures completely burned, but also that "all priests, young or old, be buried alive."[49]

The extremity of the proclamations provoked Kou to memorialize against these measures, joined by the intervening remonstration of the crown prince-regent, himself an ardent Buddhist. Failing to overturn the imperial orders, their efforts did delay their execution so that the Buddhist clerics could go into hiding. There is no account of how many were killed and how many escaped. Two years later in 448, Kou died of illness, swiftly followed by Cui. Commissioned to compile a history of the Tuoba Wei people, Cui inscribed with "an upright brush 直筆" the account on some stone tablets that did not spare their early rulers from critique of their waywardness and evil deeds. Offended, the people filed charges with the emperor, who immediately had Cui and his clan—128 members in all—executed. When Taiwu died in 452 and emperor Wencheng came to the throne, one of his first acts was an edict to revive Buddhism. Once more the region honored both traditions, and all subsequent emperors of the Wei upon their ascension would also routinely receive talismans and registers from the Daoist community. In the judgment of a modern scholar like Kenneth Ch'en, this episode represented not merely "a phase in the ideological struggle between Buddhism and Taoism," but also one "in the Sinicization of a non-Chinese people. Ts'ui, good Confucian that he was, wanted to Sinicize the T'o-pa people, and to him the foreign religion Buddhism had to be suppressed."[50] However, as the history of Chinese civilization will frequently show, violent suppression of religion, whether for fideistic or racial reason, can be a multi-edged sword. By the year 555, when emperor Wenxuan 文宣 of the Northern Qi (now the dynastic name of the region) assembled the Daoists and Buddhists for debate in his court, the loss by the former party brought on this result: "he thereby ordered that the hair of all Daoists be shaved off so that they might become śramaṇa. There were some who disobeyed, and four persons were executed. Thus all accepted the decree, and that was how the region of Qi came to be completely without Daoists."[51]

The second episode of major persecution of Buddhism again came as a result of the running conflict between Daoism and Buddhism, notably on the culturally explosive issue of priority. As early as 166, the legend that Laozi left China through the western Hangu Pass to reach India and became the Buddha to convert "the barbarians" was mentioned in a memorial to the throne by the minister Xiang Kai. By the beginning of the fourth century, the famous apocryphal sutra titled *Huahujing* 化胡經 (Conversion of the Barbarians) appeared in circulation. Numerous debates between Daoists and Buddhists would focus, among other concerns, on the various dates of birth for either Laozi or Buddha, with some Chinese advocating 687 B.C.E. for the latter while another polemicist placed Laozi's birth in 605 B.C.E. and his westward journey to convert the Buddha in 519 B.C.E. Other partisan advocates would even date Laozi to the twelfth or fifteenth century B.C.E.! Needless to say, the Buddhists wasted no time in mounting counter-arguments and refutations.[52] By the time of the episode in discussion, emperor Wudi 武帝 (r. 561–78) of the Northern Zhou began his reign disposed to permit Buddhism's continuance as usual. Nonetheless, he as a thoroughly sinicized non-Chinese was ironically unhappy with the tradition as a foreign religion. Oracular prediction of people "robed in black (黑衣)" would topple the regime that came to the court's notice added to his chagrin and misgiving, for Buddhist clerics were regularly dressed in that color. In his attempt to stamp out possible rebels associated with black, the emperor would even execute persons named Wu and Dou (homophones of black crows and black beans) and his seventh son serving as one of his attendants (homophones of seven [qi] and black varnish [qi]).[53]

The emperor's personal doubt about Buddhism's worth was abbetted by a memorial in 567 by one Wei Yuansong 衛元嵩, a native of Sichuan and a political opportunist of the first order. Though at the time of his communication with the court he was a member of the Buddhist community of Chang'an, he petitioned the throne to establish "a great all-inclusive church to embrace everyone in the populace" that would propagate the Buddhist doctrine of compassion without the encumbrance of separate monasteries and Saṅgha. The emperor, he further suggested, would become the head of his nation-wide ecclesia.[54] Although the emperor could not decide immediately to implement this proposal, his favorable reception thereof expressed itself in the appointment of Wei as the Duke of Shu (Sichuan). In the follow year, the emperor began to convene a series of debates—seven in all, lasting until 573—participated by Daoists, Confucians, and Buddhists on the priority of the Three Religions. Revealing his own preference for Confucianism, he began the assembled conference with an inaugural lecture himself on the *Record of Rites*,[55] followed by several meetings in the following months with members of the three communities engaging in intense debate and polemics. Preserved in the *Guang Hongmingji*, in fact, is an astonishing series of textual exchanges between the monk Daolin 道林 and the emperor, in which the cleric's vigorous, point-by-point objection to the the ruler's stringent critique of the faith was met by equal vehemence and meticulousness in argumentation.[56]

By 573, the emperor thought that "Confucianism must be ranked first, because it represented the traditional ideology of the land," with Daoism ranking second and Buddhism last.[57] His conviction arose in great part because of the continuous suggestions advanced by Wei, now aided by one Daoist named Zhang Bin 張賓. Stung, however, by the objections and critiques of the Buddhists, the emperor issued in 574 his decree proscribing the religion—ironically, because the debate had allegedly so exposed the weaknesses of the Daoist tradition that the emperor also authorized "the complete destruction of scriptures and images of both the Buddhist and Daoist Religions. All Śramaṇa and Daoists were to be laicized. The various licentious sacrifices and worship were thereby prohibited. Those rituals not found in canonical records would be excised."[58]

In 577, when Wudi conquered the rest of Northern Qi, he extended the proscription to all parts of north China. The emperor assembled five hundred monks and read to them in person his edict, attacking Buddhism for unfilial practice, wastage of money, and instigating revolt. As a "barbarian" faith, he further declared, it had to be destroyed by him. According to one later source, the policy of Wudi this time "destroyed all the supas, images, and shrines built by the people for several hundred years, over three million monks and nuns were returned to the laity, and over forty thousand temples were appropriated by members of the imperial family and aristocracy."[59] The trustworthiness of these figures divided the reading by two modern authorities.[60]

The third event of major imperial suppression of Buddhism, occurring during the Huichang reign period (841–46) of the Tang emperor Wuzong 武宗, is often regarded by historians as the most severe. Although the series of harsh edicts leading to appalling treatments of the clergy came within a relatively brief period of no more than six years by a young ruler who died, perhaps fortunately, before he reached age 32, the governmental action inflicted "a crippling blow" to the Saṅgha, because this persecution was also "the most widespread of its kind in China."[61] Most historians would probably share Stephen Teiser's assessment that the "unprecedented blow to Chinese Buddhist institutions" was one "from which they never fully recovered,"[62] despite the more lenient and restorative policies of the emperor Xuanzong 宣宗 (r. 847–60) that followed immediately. Another notable dimension of this particular episode is created by the fact that it had the written report of a historical—perhaps, in many instances, even an eye-witness, in the Japanese Buddhist cleric and pilgrim, Ennin 圓仁, who, as part of an appointed delegation to China, traveled throughout great parts of north and eastern China from 838 to 847. His journal provided invaluable and, sometimes, ex-

clusive information on the events of the "Huichang Ordeal,"
especially as they were experienced by the Buddhist community, corrborating and supplementing Chinese sources.[63]

One part of the imperial edict, issued in the eighth
month of 845 on "Destruction of Buddhist Monasteries and
Ordering the Laicization of Monks and Nuns 毀佛寺勒僧尼
還俗制,"[64] may be used here to illustrate some of the crucial
elements of the imperium's anti-Buddhist sentiment. As
possibly the last major pronouncement against the religion,
the ruler's hostility also reached its apposite expression by
reviving venerable grievances in the textual argument:

> We heard that before the Three Sage Dynasties, there was
> never any mentioning of Buddha, but after the Han and Wei,
> the Religion of Images (象教) arose profusely. It was the clem-
> ent season for the transmission of this alien custom and the
> profusive growth of its teachings and practices. These resulted
> in the unconscious devastation of our national character (國
> 風) and the seductive deception of human minds even as the
> common people became more deluded. Amidst the moun-
> tain ranges of the Nine Provinces and the citadels of our Two
> Capitals [for example, Chang'an and Luoyang], both the
> number of the monkish clerics and the elevation of monaster-
> ies grow by the day. They tax the strength of humans through
> their labor on craft and wood, and they rob the strength of
> humans by their making ornaments from gold and jewels. On
> the matter of due reverence and support they abandon both
> ruler and parents; on the basis of prohibitions and command-
> ments they transgress against their spouses. No other religion
> surpasses this one in wrecking the laws and injuring humans.
> Furthermore, if a single man does not plow, someone will be
> hungry because of it; if one single woman does not weave,
> someone will be cold because of it. Now, there are number-
> less monks and nuns in the empire, but they all feed while
> relying on others to farm, and they clothe themselves while
> relying on others to weave. Monasteries, temples and all living
> quarters reflect the ignorance of any rules or regulations. Their

elaborate designs and ornamentations indicate their pretension to imperial palaces and halls. That the material strength of Jin, Song, Qi, and Liang had declined and their customs became deceitful could not have been so except for this. Moreover, our Gaozu and our Taizong had used martial prowess (*wu* 武) to pacify calamitous chaos, and they had used culture (*wen* 文) to put China (華夏) in order. Holding these two sources of authority is sufficient to regulate a state. How could a puny religion of the western quarter contend with us 執此二柄，足以經邦。豈可以區區西方之教與我抗衡哉?

We should note that none of Wuzong's argument is novel. There is the chauvinistic contention that his dynasty's inherited tradition of governance is superior because it can be traced back to the antiquity of sages. There is the xenophobic contention that Buddhism is in an inferior import from an alien space. There is the ideological contention that Buddhism subverts Confucian ethics and politics. Perhaps most conspicuous of all is the economic contention that the Saṅgha embodies a huge unproductive community of consumers and wastrels of other people's labor. As has been noted in modern scholarship,[65] the protests against this aspect of Buddhism are multifaceted and of long-standing. Sidestepping the *Vinaya* proscription against all economic activities, the Chinese Saṅgha did not exist primarily as one wholly dependent on alms donated by charitable patrons. On the basis, instead, of the argument that circulation of goods would benefit the community as a whole, the ostensibly isolated temples steadily developed into large estates that were economically productive and self-sufficient. In this, their condition was enhanced frequently by lay donations and imperial patronage that brought enormous gifts of value (gold, silver, and copper that were turned into religious icons and ritual vessels), including cash. The exemption from taxes and the right to hold property both material and human (the latter include large number of slave laborers) further and decisively enhanced the Saṅgha's productive capacity. Such wealth of the temple estates built up over several centuries were undeniably at the expense of state revenue and provoked, in turn, abiding and deepening resentment from the ruler down to the lower classes of officials.

Wuzong's representative animosity towards Buddhist wealth found expression not merely in the quoted edict, for the series of harsh decrees that began from the third month of 842 was also manifestly designed, steadfastly, to strip the community from every means of economic power.[66] Throughout the turbulent next four years, there were orders for seizure of land and property (first, it was the confiscation of individual posession of coins, grain, and paddy fields, but quickly, the seizures expanded to include communal or estate holdings), the conversion of precious metals from icons and vessels for governmental use, the expulsion of unaffiliated or unregistered clergy, eventual execution of clergy without proper identification, proscription against any donation of any size to Buddhist persons or institutions, burning of scriptures, destruction of stone pillars or steles bearing Buddhist inscriptions, removal of grave monuments to priests, and massive laicization. This last aspect of those repressive measures was especially hard on "the sick, the poor, the orphaned and the aged" cared for by devout laypersons and clergy in a kind of public almshouse. The dissolution of the monasteries also victimized horrendously some 150,000 slave laborers by leaving them with neither shelter nor food.[67] The plight of the clergy, young and old, who were compelled to return to secular life on the pain of death, could be imagined readily.

What the edict quoted above did not make clear was Wuzong's life-long infatuation with Daoist teachings and practices, a predilection well-attested in the sources. He died a gruesome death apparently as a victim of ingesting poisonous drugs and pharmaceutics alleged to induce physical longevity. Beginning in 841, however, his preference nurtured already when he was only the Crown Prince manifested itself by repeatedly honoring only Daoists with a gift of royal purple robes and not the Buddhists regularly assigned to palace services during the occasions of celebrating imperial birthdays. During the years that followered, confiscated goods from monasteries were sometimes turned over to Daoist temples. At the *Yulanpen* or "ghost festival" of 844, Ennin wrote that "all of the flowers, medicines, and the like offered at the Buddha halls of the various temples [were ordered by edict to be] taken to the Hsing-t'ang kuan [Daoist Temple for the Elevation of the Tang] to be sacrificed to the Celestial Venerables [i.e., *tianzun* 天尊]."[68] The Japanese pilgrim further reported that the emperor visited the Daoist establishment the following day and summoned residents of the capital to visit, but the populace apparently resisted, while the Buddhist temples were understandably upset by the seizure of their offerings. As a grand summation of imperial achievements in cleansing the domain of the hateful religion, Wuzong's cited edict of 845 ends with these figures: "the dismantlement of more than 4,600 monasteries, the defrocking and return to taxable status of 260,500 monks and nuns, the destruction of more than 40,000 chapels and hermitages, the confiscation of 'several tens of millions' of *ch'ing* [頃] of fertile land from monastic estates, and the addition of 150,000 ex-slaves to the tax registers."[69] Stanley Weinstein was just in his assessment that this edict "provided an *ex post facto* justification for the virtual annihilation of Buddhism in China."[70]

Rehearsal of such grim episodes of imperial persecution of Buddhism returns us to a slightly earlier story of the famous scripture-pilgrim, Xuanzang, to recount a happier relationship between individual believer and state power, one that was, however, not wholly free of inherent danger or tension. His story, moreover, will be used to illumine certain problems that persist in the modern study of Chinese religions. According to the biographical writings of his disciples, Xuanzang came from a rather unusual family.[71] His grandfather Chen Kang, by scholarly excellence, was appointed Erudite in the School for the Sons of the State (*guozi boshi* 國子博士), a moderately high rank. His father Chen Hui was said to have mastered the classics at an early age and loved to be recognized as a Confucian scholar. As the Sui declined, the father buried himself in books, refusing all offers of official appointments and duties. Despite this withdrawal from public service, the paternal devotion to familial instruction in the Confucian manner never let up, and the official biography singled out one incident to praise the sensitive piety of the young Xuanzang. While reciting the paradigmatic *Classic of Filial Piety* before his father, the eight-year old suddenly rose to his feet to tidy his clothes. When asked for the reason for his abrupt action, the boy replied: "Master Zeng [Confucius's disciple] heard the voice of his teacher and arose from his mat. How could Xuanzang sit still when he hears his father's teachings?"

This anecdotal exemplum, intended surely to magnify the elite orthodoxy of both father and son, may serve at the same time as an unintended and ironic commentary of familial ethos. Given the Confucian heritage identified with ancestor, great-grandfather, grandfather, and father duly rehearsed in the biography, one would have thought that the text would proceed to provide more encomium on the acumen and achievement of the subject at hand. Xuanzang, let us notice, was indeed said to have also mastered the Confucian classics at an early age, but the account of his prodigious intelligence and love of learning becomes a mere pretext to display his astounding decision to seek "holy orders," as it were, at age thirteen. What is even more astonishing is the fact that he had an elder brother who by this time was already an ordained Buddhist priest. Of the four sons that the Chen household was said to have produced, therefore, at least two apparently had entered the Saṅgha while they were very young.

To this unusual phenomenon, the biographical text by its amazing silence implied no familial opposition. Given the strict vow of celibacy that Chinese Buddhism had always demanded of its clergy, this silence meant that the family no less than the young men themselves was willing to incur the risk of not providing a male heir for familial lineage. Xuanzang's family, in other words, could be one of those which, fully participatory (as far as we could learn from pertinent documents) in all aspects of Chinese life of their time, was also subscribing to a form of cultural diversity. They were unafraid to embrace a system of values that, in many respects, was critical of, or at odds with, their native tradition. Once the young Xuanzang had entered the Gate of Emptiness in formal commitment, we learn from the biography that he and his brother traveled widely not merely between the two Tang capitals of Chang'an and Luoyang, but also to far-away Sichuan in quest of further learning and teachings from erudite priests. Apparently, these activities during the dangerous and tumultuous period of transition between the Sui and the Tang were tacitly supported by the family.

Although we have already alluded to the considerable popularity of Buddhism in the Sui and early Tang, this religion's pervasive presence in the land was not met with universal acceptance. Even in the person of Emperor Taizong, whose own career eventually entailed such intimate involvement with this particular monk no less than with the larger monastic and lay communities, the ruler's attitude towards Buddhism was marked more by manipulations of opportunistic politics than by the urgent promptings of faith.[72] This contrast of attitude and behavior towards religion on the part of emperor and subject may betoken not merely the idiosyncratic difference of two individuals but also the wider pheonomenon of reception or resistance. In the accounts of Xuanzang's early life and already assertive engagement with Buddhist studies and preaching in fraternal company, could we not detect perhaps the family's basic and genial regard for this religion? Might not such familial hospitality, in turn, deepen his commitment to the extent of undertaking not merely the daunting pilgrminage of sixteen years to seek Buddhist scriptures in India yet unavailable to the Chinese but also the task of a reversed missionary throughout the land of his faith when he participated liberally in doctrinal disputations and evangelistic preaching? Finally, and most significantly, could such familial support furnish him with the needed courage and confidence to embark on his journey against imperial proscription, thus transforming a religious pilgrimage into also an act of religious defiance against the Chinese state?

Such questions on possible influence of familial setting are acknowledgeably rhetorical and speculative. What we know with certainty, however, was the fact that Xuanzang departed Tang territory furtively, for "at this time," declares the FSZ (1. 7), "the state's governance was new and its frontiers did not reach far. The people were prohibited from going to foreign domains." The transgressive act of the monk thus earned him a contemporary biographer's justifiable observation that he left Tang China "with a warrant on his head,"[73] but Sally Wriggin's remark only inferred the severity of his crime. The textualized accounts of his early biographers revealed more intensely his religious convictions.

The initial petition for permission to go West for scriptures and doctrinal clarification, according to FSZ 1. 6, was submitted by Xuanzang and other clerics. "When the imperial rescript denied it, all the others retreated, but the Master of the Law refused to bend (bu qu 不屈). Because he then resolved to travel alone and the road to the West was both difficult and dangerous, he had to interrogate his mind-and-heart on the matter. Since he had been able to bear and overcome so many afflictions of humankind already, he could not retreat from his present duty. Only then did he enter a stūpa to make known his firm resolve, begging in prayer for the various saints' secret benediction so that his journey and return might be unimpeded."

This depiction of the priest's resolve not only narrates the deliberateness of his motivation but also the steadfast-ness of his resolve. The biographies tell us that during the process of leaving Chinese territory, Xuanzang was warned twice about his incriminating action. The FSZ (1. 6–7) had only the briefest mention of one Li Daliang, Regional Military Commander of Liangzhou, who, upon learning of the priest's desired project, simply urged him to turn back. In the *Obituary of Xuanzang* composed by the disciple Ming-xiang most likely in 664 and thus the earliest biography of the priest, a slightly longer anecdote detailed the incident of a nameless barbarian hired to sneak the pilgrim past the five signal-fire ramparts strung out beyond the Jade-Gate Pass.

> In the middle of the night [while they were sleeping by a river bank], the barbarian arose and walked toward the Master of the Law with a drawn knife and the intent to kill him. Where-upon the Master of the Law rose up and began immediately to recite the name of the Buddha and a sūtra. The barbarian sat down again, only to stand up once more after a little while. He said to the priest:
>
> "According to the Law of the State, it is a most serious crime to go to a foreign state on your private wish. When you pass through the road beneath those five signal-fires, you will be caught for certain. Once you are arrested, you are a dead man! Since your student still has family obligations, how could I take this on myself! Imperial Law cannot be breached. Let me go back with the Master."

The Master of the Law replied, "Xuanzang can only die facing the West, but I vow I shall not return East and live. If my patron cannot do this, he is free to turn back. Let Xuanzang proceed by himself."[74]

Though redolent of hagiographic hyperbole, this short tale also rings true at another level with dramatic irony. For the priest stubbornly committed to his journey to the West, it took a barbarian (*hu*) to remind a Tang subject of his own social reality to which both of them were subject, and to point out both the nature and risk of his illicit action. The word I translated as "private wish" is *si* 私, a word as old as the *Classic of Documents*; its meaning stretches through Warring States texts (for example, *Analects*, *Laozi*, *Mencius*, *Lüshi chunqiu*) to the Han compendium *Record of Rites* to denote all that is personal, self-regarding, self-directed, and self-motivated.[75] In pre-modern China's rigid taxonomy of both social structures and human affects, whatever is outside the domain of state governance and power (*gong*) is *si*, including even clan or household kin (for example, *Zuo Commentary*, Duke Xuan 17). Whatever is human motive or action not originating from the state or, in a household or clan, parental authority or authorization, is *si*, and thus private desire and personal possession—inclusive of space and time—always exist in the parlous potential of selfishness. This predominantly negative assessment of the personal, in fact, is what led eventually to the escalating debate on *gong* and *si* among the many Ming-Qing Confucian elites when they began to question, ever so cautiously, the origin, maintenance, and limit of imperial power.[76] To the Tang barbarian, however, the Chinese priest's act of seeking the Dharma in the West, however noble, still falls within the realm of the private and thus violates the law of the state that brooks no rivalry.

Against the state's initial refusal of travel permission and the specific warning by the barbarian recounted in the two biographies, Xuanzang's resistance is portrayed in a language normally reserved in Chinese writings for exemplary political subjects. The FSZ says that the priest refused to bow or bend (*bu qu*), a phrase recalling the defiant posture of countless patriots celebrated for their undying loyalism when threatened with death by execution or other means. His own words represented in the *Obituary* indicates that he was clearly ready to pay the supreme sacrifice for the decision of seeking scripture. Confronting the extreme danger of losing his life to a barbarian desperate to uphold the law of the Tang (what profound textual irony!), Xuanzang significantly never attempted to justify his undertaking in terms of what great boon he was hoping to obtain for his nation or even his people. His passionate commitment to his long, hazardous pilgrimage and its stupendous achievements, in any final assessment, must be honored and recognized first and foremost as an act of religious devotion. That kind of motivation, regretably, has often been lost on modern Chinese savants writing on the very persons and topics of the Buddhist tradition. Thus, so learned and dedicated an investigator as Liang Qichao could declare: "The people of our nation who went westward to seek the Dharma were not like Christians who made their pilgrimages to Jerusalem or Muslims to Mecca, for those performed their worship purely out of superstition. Chinese motivation stemmed entirely from scholarship, for all our pilgrims were dissatisfaied with the indirect Buddhist learning of the Western territories or the partial views of one particular denomination."[77] Thus, Hu Shi also was fond of calling Xuanzang "China's first overseas student (*di yi ge Zhongguo liuxue sheng*)," and the epithet has been used many times since.

Although the intellectual acumen and accomplishment of Xuanzang cannot be denied, to treat him only as a scholar is to miss both the power of his person and the significance of his undertaking. Trained first in Confucian ethics and politics to revere without reservation both sovereign and the state, Xuanzang nonetheless by his action indicated his belief that there was a demand, a summons, and a law that were higher than any norm or form of authority sanctioned by his native tradition. His thoughts, words, and deeds recorded in those early segments of his biographies were as "scandalous" as the sixth-century Parthian dumping all his wealth into a river after he heard Buddhist preaching, for neither motivation could find adequate explanation in strictly secular terms.[78] For to think, as Xuanzang the young Buddhist zealot obviously did, that Buddhist writings were necessary to the welfare and fulfilment of the Chinese people (that was the real crux of the need for doctrinal clarification that Liang Qichao failed to acknowledge accurately) is in essence to deny the self-sufficiency or adequacy of indigenous wisdom and thought, and to identify one's deepest norms and values with something regarded (in the rhetoric of anti-Buddhist polemics) as non-Chinese. To affirm that the Buddhist Saṅgha should supercede the obligations of one's family, as the younger teenager Xuanzang also maintained when he sought ordination at the Luoyang monastery (FSZ 5. 2–3), is to tear apart the ties of kinship that Chinese had valued since time immemorial. Finally, to insist that such objects of one's religious veneration (for example, Buddhist scriptures and doctrines) as something to be sought without regard for even imperial prohibition is to incur the crime of treason. Like the early Christians' refusal to worship Caesar because of their faith that found expression in the assertion, "*Kyrios Christos* or Christ is Lord," Xuanzang's actions—from his youthful dedication, through secret defiance of royal command, to prolonged endurance of hardship on his journey— were wrought and sustained by religious zeal. Over the long stretches of history before and after this famous pilgrim, the Saṅgha might have indeed "come to terms" by and large with "the supremacy of the state" as Professor Ch'en had written, but there would always be the exception of individual conviction and commitment.

The story of this individual's daring and potentially incriminating action based on religious faith, as we all know, had a happy ending. Smart enough to have sent envoys ahead of him to seek imperial pardon before he set foot again on Tang territory upon his return with scriptures, the reception and exaltation Xuanzang received for the rest of his life from the emperors and imperial household had ample documentation. Indeed, it was the unstinting imperial patronage and support that enabled him to bequeath eventually to the Chinese people in their own script 75 volumes or 1,341 scrolls of new Buddhist writings, surpassing the accomplishment of any scriptural translator in previous Chinese history and never repeated since. For each Xuanzang who met with such good fortune, however, one wonders how many named and nameless practitioners of religion in historical China would suffer a different fate, when their beliefs and actions ran afoul of the unacknowledged and unchallenged premises of state religion.

6

An Inconclusive Conclusion

*T*HE QUESTION posed at the end of the last chapter returns us conveniently to the present situation in China with which we began our study. We recall what historian of religions Daniel Overmyer had described as "a protracted policy of containment through recognition, incorporation (bestowing imperial placards, official registration of cults), and co-option (endorsing worship of 'local heroes and personified spirits')" that had persisted from the Han down to the Ming and Qing,[1] to which we must add that that policy frequently included outright persecution, banning, and destruction of both human lives and property. In that light, the overthrow of the imperial form of governance in the first Republican revolution of 1911 was momentous not only as a political event. In terms of the fortunes of religion, the republican ideals and aspirations could also signal an unprecedented revolution far more significant and consequential than even the political transformation. For, those ideals and aspirations were supposedly directed towards the establishment of a truly democratic and secular government, that, despite some nostalgic reformers had wanted at the time to re-instate Confucianism as an official state religion. Eventually, Article 13 of the Constitution of the Republic of China adopted by the National Assembly and promulgated by the government in 1947 states unambiguously that "the people shall have freedom of religious belief."[2] This assertion, however, does not mean that the newly formed Chinese republic or its eventual Communist successor abstained from intervention in the nation's religious affairs and traditions. Because the unprecedented attempt to create an entirely new form of government for one of the oldest continuous civilizations was fueled by the all-consuming passion for modernization, elite leaders of nearly all stripes of political persuasion almost inevitably were driven to engage religion in one way or another.

Sharing the traditional Confucian's contempt for both popular religions and even the more developed forms and doctrines of Daoism and Buddhism, the vast majority of modern Chinese intellectuals tend to regard religion as virtually synonymous with "superstition," a debilitating and decadent remnant of all that was bad with the old Chinese culture that should be swept away in whole or in large part. Even political reactionaries who might have been tempted by certain dictatorial, if not imperial, pretensions were campaigning against religion (particularly in the form of local institutions and customs) in the early decades of the republic.[3] Deeply aware of how various groups and movements of religious dissenters throughout Chinese history often ended as political rebels and revolutionaries, the Chinese Nationalists or *Kuomintang* banned all "redemptive societies" once they achieved consolidated power after Chiang Kai-shek's successful northern expedition of 1928.[4] Various governmental agencies such as the Ministry of the Interior and the Bureau of Social Affairs oversaw a number of either established ecclesiastical organization like the Buddhist Association of the Republic of China and other less known ones. Sporadic campaigns against religions like Christianity and Buddhism also enjoyed official sanction during the decade of the twenties.[5] Despite Christianity's checkered political history in China since the seventeenth century, one associated paradoxically with both Western imperialism and the effective introduction of new culture (educational, scientific, and political) to China, first- and second-generation leaders of the KMT tended to exploit that religion continuously for their own profit. Throughout his revolutionary struggles against the Manchu govenment, Sun Yat-sen found shelter and support from missionaries and Christian congregations overseas both Chinese and non-Chinese. Chiang Kai-shek himself promoted different political movements that adroitly blended Confucian tenets with Christian teachings. During the protracted struggle against the Japanese and later against the Communists, Madame Chiang's Christian profession and polemics provided probably the single most effective instrument in swaying Western public opinion, especially in the United States.

After World War II, Taiwan's retrocession first as a province of China only to become the island nation ruled by the defeated Nationalists in 1949 added unexpected twists and turns in the relationship between state and religion in that particular Chinese society. The KMT's autocratic governance of the first two decades yielded eventually to the rapid modernization, economic expansion, and political liberalization during the late 1980s that simultaneously deepened the rule of law and broadened the independence of the press. This process, in turn, heralded unprecedented liberty for the practice of religion, including the most dramatic revitalization of the Buddhist Saṅgha in a contemporary Asian community. The economic prowess of this religion on Taiwan manifested itself in the proliferation of educational institutions and eleemosynary agencies under its sponsorship. Their world-wide impact in social and relief work and health care also now directly measures "the freedom of religion" increasingly realized as a constitutional right of the island's citizens. That freedom extends beyond established traditions of Daoism and Buddhism to encourage the prosperous flourishing of distinctive local deities, temples, and movements.[6]

If Christianity has had a peculiar alliance with the early leaders of the KMT, it has functioned also ironically to undermine and, eventually, to undo—at least through the ballot box—the Nationalists' monolithic grip on power. Although that religion was introduced to the island through Dutch settlers in the seventeenth century, sustained and effective Christian presence came with Canadian Presbyterian missionaries during the nineteenth. Their ministry carried out in local congregations, schools, and hospitals had produced a lasting impact on the native Taiwanese, to such extent that many of their current leaders in the Democratic Progress Party (currently occupying the presidential mansion) are Christians. Lee Teng-hui, the Cornell-trained agricultural economist who was elected as Taiwan's first native-born president in 1990 under the KMT banner but eventually left the party upon retirement, used to invite severe criticism and ridicule from news media and political opponents alike for lacing his speeches with too many biblical allusions and comparisons of himself to Moses.

Unlike the people of contemporary Taiwan, Chinese religious adherents on the mainland, though making significant gains during the recent decade, face a much steeper uphill struggle in acquiring greater freedom to practice their beliefs, if only because the central state government is committed to a manifestly different political ideology and ruling structure.[7] The Chinese Communist Party (CCP) that triumphed in 1949 and went on to establish the People's Republic of China (PRC) is, as we have noted in the beginning of this book, unambiguous in its espousal of classic Marxist profession of atheism.

> Citizens of the PRC enjoy freedom of religious belief. No state organ, public organization or individual may compel citizens to believe in, or not to believe in, any religion: nor may they discriminate against citizens who believe in, or do not believe in, any religion. The state protects normal religious activities. No one may make use of religion to engage in activities that disrupt public order, impair the health of citizens or interfere with the educational system of the state. Religious bodies and religious affairs are not subject to any foreign domination.[8]

The famous "Document 19" we alluded to at the beginning also expands the Party's understanding of religion by attributing its development to the primitive period of "low level of production" when people allegedly were held in awe by natural phenomena. Although the Constitution allows for religion to exist in China, it is to be understood as a necessary concession, strictly provisional and temporary, to the poor economic and educational condition of the vast majority of her citizens. The CCP, however, is committed to rid China's religious traditions and communities from their "erroneous" ties to the "feudal" past and the complete severance from any link to colonial or imperialistic agencies from abroad. No party members, in fact, are permitted to be followers of any religion (a *prima facie* contradiction to the universal guarantee specified in the Constitution). This has been, parenthetically, one specially galling offense committed by the sectarian movement called Falun Gong (literally, Merit of the Dharma Wheel) that, though condemned and outlawed on the mainland, seems to be very active worldwide. At its initial phase of conflict with the central government, what alarmed political leaders was the discovery that many party members, including retired officials both civil and military, belonged to the group.

The confident official assertion that "religion will eventually disappear from human history"[9] may astonish readers from Western nations who routinely regard the "free exercise" of their religious beliefs as a proper right to be guaranteed and enjoyed, but the 1982 declarations of the Chinese government already represented a significant advance from the brutal suppression and ruthless campaigns against religion in the first three decades of the PRC. In that period of rampant and repeated Maoist incitation for the dictator's fanatical followers to stamp out everything deemed the refuse of a decadent past or a hated bequest of foreign cultures, practitioners of all religions were persecuted. There was wholesale laicization of Buddhist and Daoists priests and nuns along with Catholic clergy, and there were indiscriminate jailing and execution of Confucian "reactionaries" and Christian traitors. Forced marriages of laicized clergy were also routinely imposed.[10] Countless religious edifices were destroyed and land owned by different communities confiscated. Only after Mao Zedong's death in 1976 did the nation gradually return to a more civil and tolerant form of government.

In China today, all religious groups and movements must be formallly registered with the Bureau of Religious Affairs (with national offices in Beijing and provincial and municipal branches throughout the country) directly under the supervision of the CCP and certified to be "patriotic" before they can operate legally. The major religions thus recognized are Daoism, Buddhism, Islam, Christian Catholicism, and Christian Protestantism. Although each of these traditions appears to be enjoying a measure of growth and security undreamt of during the Maoist era, each also faces problems with the state that are peculiar to its own ethos and history. Religious Daoism, as already noted, arose in the Han as political dissenters who sought to overthrow the imperial government by force. Historically, it has always been a religion intimately connected to regional sympathies and local pieties, thereby perennially incurring suspicion and hostility from the central government. Despite imperial patronage in different dynastic and reign periods, Daoism's frequent alliance or cooperation with sectarian movements and uprisings led to regular suppressions. The abrogation of priestly ordination ordered by the late Qing government and repeated under both National and Communist rule was repealed and priestly ordination was permitted to resume only in the late 1980s.[11]

As for Buddhism, many temples have been re-opened and allowed to operate, and the number of clergy has been slowly permitted to increase. The woeful lack of educational facilities in turn creates serious hardships for the training of clerical and lay leadership, and the stigma of Buddhism's essentially foreign origin is at the moment compounded manyfold by the contentious and acrimonious situation in Tibet.[12] A religious tradition's tie to foreign communities is almost an invitation to skeptical scrutiny by the government on its "patriotic" qualification and its independence from foreign domination. Thus Islam, usually identified with "ethnic minorities" of the nation, can be suspected of abetting seditious efforts to "divide the motherland." The particular conflict with the Roman Catholic Church since the inception of the PRC, revolving inevitably around the thorny question of the clergy's allegiance to a foreign papacy, has never been resolved despite ernest attempts at formal relations by the Vatican. Even now, this denomination with significant growth in the numbers of its congregation (current estimate approaches thirty-five million) must face the anomaly of being run by a "legal" Church, whose priests are ordained by the state, and an "underground" ecclesia, one whose clergy remain secretly loyal to the Pope. Protestant Christianity, ostensibly less vulnerable to the liabilities of foreign alliances, can be hampered in any church-growth efforts because of severe constraints on the recruitment and education of its clergy. Congregations and believers of a more evangelical persuasion will encounter suppressive measure no different from those meted out to the followers of Falun Gong.

At the close of this brief study of state and religion in China from the perspective of history and texts, the inevitable further question occasioned by our investigation concerns the exercise of religious liberty as a desired human right. Put another way, do fundamental rights universally conceived include the right to believe and practice religion? The discourse of liberal thought in the West since the time of the Enlightenment would like to answer in ringing affirmation, but I should point out that the regard for the individual's well-being against all forms of collectivism and authoritarianism does not necessarily uphold such an inference. Whether the fulfilment of life that each individual is posited to be desirious of and entitled to encompasses *necessarily* the desire to believe and act religiously depends on one's ideal of what ought to be the meaning of that fulfilment. The ideal is a product of philosophical anthropology that may or may not include religion as an indispensable constitutive component.

Taken not entirely in context, the words of the PRC's Constitution—that her citizens are guaranteed "the right to believe" as much as "the right not to believe"—may betoken on the surface an admirable, even-handed ideal of neutrality to which all free and secular societies should aspire. The tradition of the West since the dawn of the early modern era, on the other hand, has for the most part sought to uphold fully "the innate and lively decorum of a truly secular community that respects truly religious people."[13] The question that must be asked in reverse in our current global situation is whether "truly religious people" of whatever stripe and persuasion are likely to appreciate such "decorum" sufficiently to permit unfettered and uncontested existence of "a truly secular community" as one constituted innately by diverse religiosities. No doubt, the hope that a truly secular community could respect religion and allow it to flourish freely has been nurtured in the West as much by its undeniable religious heritage as by the nobility of its political and social thought. As long as religious convictions and people do not threaten the basis of secular, civil society, religion will be free—including continuous and even illicit attempts to intrude into the very process and structure of governance. Thus in the practical arena of historical life, the entanglement and often conflict with religion occurs incessantly and unavoidably on a daily basis—at the largest

communal level or the smallest individual one, on matters of national security or of personal whim (for example
a US chief justice at the state court level displaying the ten
commandments in his courtroom). When "a fundamental-
ist Muslim organisation unexpectedly won a large number
of seats in an election for [France's] first national council of
Muslims," the French interior minister immediately threatened to expel such leaders and "make sure that the council would not be used to spread views that run counter to
French values, particularly the promotion of Islamic law."[14]
With the continuous buildup of an alien Islamic presence
through the escalating influx of immigrants, the residents
of Cergy le Haut, France, are now wondering whether
buildings with minarets will eventually dominate a town of
conspicuous church steeples.[15] After the complaint by Adel
Smith, a Muslim activist, in reaction to which a court in
the central city of L'Aquila acted to remove the display of
crucifixes in a primary school of the city, Italian government
ministers and cardinals lined up to protest such removal of
"a symbol of the basic values of our country."[16]

Religious symbols—whether pictorial, iconic, or sartorial—and their public display have nonetheless acquired a
new sense of controversy in the light of the current development of dress code in French public schools. To re-affirm
the binding principle of political secularism established
by the legislation of 1905, the report on education to the
French President from a special committed chaired by
Bernard Stasi begins with the unequivocal declaration that
"secularity is constitutive of our entire collective history (*la
laïcité est constitutive de notre histoire collective*)." In context, the document argues that "our" means the history of
virtually the entire span of Western history, with the conspicuous absence of any mention of the Hebrew civilization.[17] Based on the report, President Jacques Chirac has
lent his support for the Assembly to pass a new law in 2004

to ban "'conspicuous' religious symbols in French public schools—large crosses for Christians, head scarves for Muslim girls, or skullcaps for Jewish boys."[18] Two months later, the French action, as a patent form of "benign" secularism that may well threaten the free exercise of religion and conscience, was noted by the U.S. Supreme Court Justice Antonin Scalia in his dissent from the majority ruling on allowing the states to withhold college scholarships from students preparing for religious ministry.[19] These examples, admittedly annoying and aggravating, represent perhaps only minor and manageable conflicts. When, however, such conflicts expand exponentially into large scale armed violence, as in the current war "against terrorism" undertaken by the United States and taken to Afghanistan and Iraq, the depth and scope of religion's embroilment in politics are not only immeasurable and inseparable, but each side of the adversarial situation also mirrors exactly the other in the most vitriolic language and hostile action.[20]

Returning to the Chinese side of the discussion about the state and religion, we should remember that its commitment to exercise a firm grip on all matters pertaining to the religious life of her people remains as unyielding and totalizing as ever despite the worded guarantee found in the Constitution. Indeed, during the immediate past few years, as Pitman Potter has so carefully reported in his *CQ* essay, the concern with managing China's religious affairs has occupied the highest national leaders at such a level of frequency and intensity that it far surpasses any comparable efforts on the part of Western governments. In spite of recorded meetings by the highest echelon of governmental leaders, however, the implications of religious commitment to state ideology in China's imperial past and the state's self-understanding of what constitutes legitimate power are questions that are seldom pondered even by contemporary Chinese intellectuals, let alone by the political leaders. To predict constitutionally the certain disappearance of religions from history is at the very least a form of blatant ideological commitment that can and should be disputed, but *to declare that the state can know and define what are "normal religious activities" is itself to advance a religious claim.* Any deviation from the norms set by the state—whether the practice of Falun Gong or sacerdotal submission to the Roman papacy—is bound to incur governmental censorship and suppression, because the ancient sin of disloyalty (*bu zhong*) is now supplanted by the crime of being unpatriotic (*bu aiguo*). The imperial state cult might have been abolished through political revolution, but a large part of its mentality, its cultic obsession with state power and legitimacy propped up by a particular form of ideology, remains intact. Why should political power be conceived of only as a particular party's *permanent* possession is not merely never questioned; it is also presumed and asserted with dogmatic certainty.

The People's Republic, in my view, is using religion to police and regulate religion, just as the imperial state had done for more than two millennia. Despite the adoption of a constitution that allegedly would transform its sociopolitical body into a modern, secular republic, it has yet to scrutinize and query the legitimacy of its enduring form of political religion—the worship of absolute power invested in the state. The ongoing controversy over governance in the newly reclaimed territory of Hong Kong and its pace of permissible democratic reforms significantly reveals the pitfalls of entrenched conviction. Confronted by rising popular demand to accelerate the adoption of plenary suffrage, the Beijing government as of this writing, resorts, among other measures, to reiterate ever more vocally the proclamation by Deng Xiaoping that only "patriots"—which is to say, those who wholeheartedly support "the motherland's restoration of its sovereignty over Hong Kong" are fit to rule

Hong Kong.[21] This announced policy of the PRC on the former colony is certainly consistent with other known policies, to say the least, because constitutionally only patriots are fit to enjoy the freedom to believe, including the religion supposedly of their own choosing. However, reigning supreme over all other beliefs must be unsullied nationalism, the unquestionable belief in the country, "the ancestral state (*zu guo* 祖國)." This Chinese nomenclature of national self-reference—perhaps even more revealing than such other terms exalting political collectivity and unity as "fatherland," "motherland," and "melting pot"—tallies well with the imperial ideology of Chinese history. Although ancestral cults by themselves may be understood as "exclusive rather than inclusive, [for] they tend to represent selfish and sectional interests and the conflict over them, and affect power divisions and classificatory distinctions within and among political groups,"[22] there is little ambiguity in imperial China once the ruler has gained accession. By his own submission to his designated ancestors, in principle regarded as all inclusive, the emperor would at the same time acquire absolute power over all his subjects. Small wonder that the Han emperor Yuandi 元帝 (r. 48–32 B.C.E.) could declare at the beginning of his reign: "We make it a point to establish personally our ancestral temple, because this is the ultimate power to build up our authority, eliminate the sprouts of rebellion, and make the people one 所親以立宗廟，蓋建威，銷萌，一民之至權也."[23] Similarly, the constant appeal of the contemporary state for the Chinese communities, whether on native soil or in diaspora, to be patriotic represents a none-too-subtle wielding of the instrument of control. The ancestral state is, after all, still a totalitarian state, one which, in its demand for total and unconditional submission, exists to make the people one (*yimin*) by erasing all differences—whether ethnic, cultural, political, and linguistic.

In the contentious dialogue with China these days, it seems to me that simply reporting Chinese represssive policies and using such reports to try to compel the government to alter them will hardly produce magical results. A more difficult but potentially more enabling tactic of conversation is to urge the Chinese elites to re-examine their understanding of the nature and basis of state power no less than that of religion, and to come to terms as well with their historical devolution and contemporary exercise. That kind of undertaking should be obligatory also for the West, for its discourse on liberal democracy too frequently appears to assume that there need be no essential opposition between two fundamental affirmations—that the human is a religious being (*homo religiosus*) and that "man by nature is a political animal (*ho anthrōpos physei politikon zōov*)" (Aristotle, *Politics* 1253a). How compatible these two views truly are will, in fact, test daily the fabric of social, political, and religious life of any civil community, for their collison will incite one's profoundest passion and verify that person's deepest commitment. In the United States, for example, the struggle to maintain the delicate balance between the interests implicated in the Establishment Clause of her Constitution and those in the Free Exercise Clause provides a neverending trial of judicial sagacity. In view of the perplexity stemming from conflicting ideals in liberal democracy and from the disparity between those ideals and their realization in society, neither Americans nor Europeans should be too smug in their colloquy with the Chinese on politics and religion.

NOTES

NOTES TO CHAPTER 1

1. The two citations are taken from Donald E. MacInnis, *Religion in China Today: Policy and Practice* (Maryknoll: Orbis, 1989), p. 10. This kind of characterization directed toward archaic religious beliefs and practices of Chinese antiquity is widespread among Chinese scholars, and the implicitly Darwinian tendency to label religious phenomena as "primitive" or "superstitious" is readily discernible in many studies, not all of them by Marxist scholars. In his *Zhongguo sixiangshi dagang* 中國思想史大綱 [An Outline of the History of Chinese Religious Thought] (Taibei: Taiwan Zhonghua shuju, 1977), for example, Wang Zhixin 王治心 has argued in his introductory chapter (pp. 1–24) that ancient Han religion(s) were more "practically" oriented because of the agrarian culture of the central plains, as contrasted with the "mystical theories 玄理思想 of the barbarous Southeast" and the "nihilism 虛無主義" later imported through Buddhism. On the widespread popularity of "shamanism 巫術," a topic of enormous controversy these days among China specialists, Wang thinks that its primary reason is attributable to the "immaturity of the people's intelligence 民智的幼稚" (p. 23)!

2. MacKinnis, p. 15, with emphasis added.

3. *Ibid.*, p. 15.

4. *Ibid.*, p. 10.

5. "Country Reports on Human Rights Practices—2001" for China (Includes Hong Kong and Macau) and Released by the Bureau of Democracy, Human Rights, and Labor on March 4th, 2002, p. 3 of 77. The report may be found in http://www.state.gov/g/drl./rls.hrrpt/2001/eap/8289pf.htm.

6. *The New York Times* (August 10th, 2001), p. A8.

7. C.K. Yang, *Religion in Chinese Society: A Study of Contemporary Social functions of Religion and Some of Their Historical Factors* (Berkeley: University of California Press, 1967), p. 104.

8. *Ibid.*, p. 105, citing Joachim Wach, *Sociology of Religion* (Chicago: University of Chicago Press, 1944), Chapter VII.

9. See Zhang Rongming 张荣明, *Zhongguo di guojiao: cong shanggu dao Dong Han* 中国的国教: 从上古到东汉 (Beijing: Zhongguo shehui kexue chubanshe, 2001).

NOTES TO CHAPTER 2

1. See W.E. Soothill, *The Three Religions of China* (London: Hodder and Stoughton, 1913), p. 6. More recently, it has been noted in Lydia H. Liu, *Translingual Practice: Literature, National Culture, and Translated Modernity—China, 1900–1937* (Stanford: Stanford Unviersity Press, 1995), pp. 259–378 [Appendixes]. Not all modern Chinese neologisms came from Japan, for both earlier Catholic and late imperial Protestant missionaries contributed to such a linguistic development. See Federico Masini, *The Formation of Modern Chinese Lexicon and Its Evolution toward a National Language: The Period from 1840 to 1898* (Berkeley: University of California, Berkeley, 1993).

2. See Guo Zhanbo 郭湛波, *Jindai Zhongguo shi* 近代中國史 (Hong Kong: Longmen shuju, 1973), pp. 124–25: "Confucius discussed only humans and not ghosts or spirits, only life and not death. This was not just Confucius's personal preference, for China fundamentally had no religion. Religions in China all came from outside, like Buddhism, Islam, and Christianity. . . . Take the *Classic of Change*, one of the earliest books of China. It has profound truths, but they lack a religious character. . . . What, we may ask, is the Great Ultimate (*taiji*)? It is a principle and not a god. The *Classic of Documents* and *Classic of Poetry* often speak of 'Heaven (*tian*)' and 'High God (*shangdi*)' but such terms are used to address humans. The discourse on clan laws and ancestor worship stipulates that ancestors are to be revered as Heaven, and hence the teaching that 'there is no greater filial piety than the sacrifice to Heaven [an allusion to the *Liji* or *Record of Rites*].' Even this is not religion." All translations in this study, unless otherwise indicated, are my own.

3. See Wilhelm Grube, *Religion und Kultus der Chinesen* (Leipzig: Rudolf Haupt, 1910), for notions and descriptions of traditional Chinese society that directly anticipate Weber.

4. Max Weber, *The Religion of China: Confucianism and Taoism*, trans. and ed. Hans H. Gerth (New York: Free Press, 1951), pp. 156–57. Even as astute a student of pre-modern Chinese letters as David Hawkes could assert, early in his career, that "the word secular tends to recur when one speaks in general terms about Chinese literature—or, for that matter, about Chinese society. Imperial China may be likened to a medieval European society without Christianity in which all, not only half, the ruling class were clerks. The immense esteem in which literacy and education were held meant that a great deal of literary activity was patronized and institutionalized by the state." See his entry on "Literature," in *The Legacy of China*, ed. Raymond Dawson (Oxford: Clarendon, 1964), pp. 86–87. In the light of more current research on pre-modern Chinese society, the question provoked by such an observation is: what should we say if the vast majority of those clerks were believers and practitioners of a form of religiosity that cannot be measured by Christianity?

5. Joseph Needham, with the collaboration of Wang Ling and Lu Gwei-djen, *Science and Civilisation in China*, 4 pt. 3 (Cambridge: At the University Press, 1971): 90, note a.

6. See Huang Zunxian, *Ribenguo zhi* 日本國志 (Shanghai: Tushu jicheng yinshuguan, 1898; facs. rpt Taibei: Wenhai, 1974), 32:11a; Liang Qichao, "Lun zhina zongjiao gaige 論支那宗教改革," in *Yinbing shi heji-wenji* 飲冰室和集文集 (24 vols. Shanghai: Zhonghua shuju, 1936), 1: 54–60.

7. For the reference to *san jiao*, see Matteo Ricci, S.J., *The True Meaning of The Lord of Heaven* (T'ien-chu Shih-i 天主實義), A Chinese-English Edition ed. Edward J. Malatesta, S.J. (St. Louis: The Institute of Jesuit Sources in cooperation with The Ricci Institute Taipei, Taiwan, 1985), ch. 2, p. 98. For *Tianzhu zhengjiao*, see ch. 6, p. 342. For a provocative study of Ricci's evangelistic and apologetic tactics, see Lionel M. Jensen, *Manufacturing Confucianism: Chinese Traditions and Universal Civilization* (Durham: Duke University Press, 1997), Part One. See also Wang Xiaochao, *Christianity and Imperial Culture: Chinese Christian Apologetics in the Seventeenth Century and*

their Latin Patristic Equivalent (Leiden: Brill, 1998); René Etiemble, *Les Jesuites en Chine: la querrelle des rites (1552–1773)* (Paris: René Julliard, 1966); Jacques Gernet, *China and the Christian Impact: A Conflict of Cultures,* trans. Janet Lloyd (Cambridge: Cambridge University Press, 1985); D.E. Mungello, *Curious Land: Jesuit Accommodation and the Origins of Sinology* (Honolulu: University of Hawaii Press, 1985); Li Shanxiu 李善修, *Tianzhujiao zhongguohua zhi tantao* 天主教中國化之探討 (Taizhong: Guanqi chubanshe, 1976); Lin Jinshui 林金水, *Li Madou yu Zhongguo* 利瑪竇與中國 (Beijing: Zhongguo shehui kexue chubanshe, 1996); Lin Zhiping 林治平, ed., *Jidujiao yu Zhongguo bensehua* 基督教與中國本色化 (Taibei: Yuzhou guang chubanshe, 1990); Willard J. Peterson, "Learning from Heaven: The Introduction of Christianity and Other Western Ideas into Late Ming China," in *The Cambridge History of China,* Vol. 8, eds. Denis Twitchett and Frederick Mote (Cambridge: Cambridge University Press, 1998), pp. 789–839; Yves Raguin, "Das Problem der Inkulturation und der chinesische Ritenstreit," in *Ignationisch: Eigenart und Methode der Gesellschaft Jesu,* ed. Michael Sievernish und Günter Switek (Freiburg: Herder, 1990), pp. 272–292; Paul Rule, *K'ung-tzu or Confucius: The Jesuit Interpretation of Confucianism* (Sydney: Allen and Unwin Australia, 1986); Sun Shangyang 孫尚揚, *Jidujiao yu Mingmo Ruxue* 基督教與明末儒學 (Beijing: Dongfang chubanshe, 1994).

8. Wing-tsit Chan, *Religious Trends in Modern China* (New York: Columbia University Press, 1953), p. 16, emphasis added. See also Wilfred Cantwell Smith, *The Meaning and End of Religion* (Minneapolis: Fortress Press, 1962). For more recent debates, see Huang Jinxing [Chin-shing] 黃進興, "Zuowei zongjiao di Rujiao: yi ge bijiao zongjiao di chubu tantao 作為宗教的儒教: 一個比較宗教的初步探討," in *Yazhou yanjiu* 亞洲研究 (July 1997): 184–223; Ren Jiyu 任继愈, ed., *Rujiao wenti zhenglun ji* 儒教问题爭论集 (Beijing: Zongjiao wenhua chubanshe, 2000).

9. See Iichi Oguchi小口偉一 and Ichirō Hori 堀一郎, eds., *Shūkyō gaku jiten* 宗教学辞典 (Tokyo: Tokyo Daigaku Shuppankai, 1973), p. 256.

10. See "Introduction" in *Ningen to shūkyo: kindai nihonjin no shūkyōkan* 人間と宗教: 近代日本人の宗教觀, eds. Takashi Koizumi 小

泉仰, et al. (Tokyo: Toyo bunka, 1982), pp. 17–25. A more thorough discussion of the contribution of Meiji religious thought and vocabulary to the development of the modern Chinese concept *zongjiao* may be found in Chen Xiyuan 陳熙遠, "'Zongjiao—yi ge Zhongguo jindai wenhuashi shang di guanjian ci 「宗教」——一個中國近代文化史上的關鍵詞," *Xin shixue* 新史學 13/4 (December 2002): 37–54. Chen's compendious and informative account of this segment of "translingual" history cites more Japanese references. My only criticism is that his discussion overlooks the importance of different sources of religious writings that fund the Japanese linguistic decisions. Meiji writers were responding manifestly to the necessity of finding appropriate words to translate "religion" and "theology," since they were dealing with cultural phenomena (education, schools, evangelistic proselytism) of America and the European West. But to accomplish their goal, they were most likely scanning sources from Chinese texts no less than from the Buddhist canon, writings that occupy so much of their own attention on what they understood to be "religion" down through the centuries.

11. See *Zhouli Zhengzhu* 周禮鄭註 (*SBBY* edition), 18.

12. I summarize here the key glosses recorded in Tetsuji Morohashi 諸橋轍次, ed., *Dai Kan-Wa jiten* 大漢和辞典 (13 vols. Tokyo: Taishuan shoten, 1955–60), 3: 3228, collated further with those recorded in the *Hanyu da cidian* 漢語大詞典 (12 vols. Hong Kong: Joint Publishing Co., 1987), 3: 1347–48.

13. The term "state cult" as it is used in this study follows the description by John K. Shryock of a "tradition" firmly established already in the time of Confucius, which "recognized a feudal government headed by the Song of Heaven, and an upper class which was governed by an elaborate system of rules of behavior. This social and political organization was reflected in religion. The spirits of the dead, nature divinities, and political deities like the gods of the Land and Grain, were arranged under a supreme god, who by the time of the Chou was called Heaven [*tian* 天] or the Emperor on High [i.e., *shangdi* 上帝]; and just as all important decisions and policies were assumed to originate in the will of the ruler, so in the *Book of History* all the events of history show the will of Heaven." See his *The Origin*

and Development of the State Cult of Confucius, An Introductory Study (New York and London: The Century Co., 1932), pp. 4–5.

14. *Laozi zhuyi ji pingjie* 老子注譯及評介, ed. and trans., Chen Guying 陳鼓應 (Beijing: Zhonghua shuju, 1984), p. 326.

15. See *Chuang-tzu: The Seven Inner Chapters and other writings from the book*, trans. A.C. Graham (London: Allen and Unwin, 1981), p. 84.

16. It should be remembered that the reference to "Heaven and Earth [*tiandi* 天地]" in a thinker like Zhuangzi is one alluding to what is natural, a concept that is fundamentally at variance with the socio-political "Heaven" exalted by the state cult ideology and later Confucian orthodoxy. That orthodoxy assimilated and systematized the beliefs about Heaven from an ancient text like the *Classic of Poetry*, in which the meaning of a concept like *tian* ranges from a name for the astronomical heavens or sky (for example "The Three Planets appear in the sky 三星在天"—Legge, 179) to a transcendent power able and willing to dispense special blessings and assistance to select human leaders and communities (for example, Legge 375, 541, 575) or afflict them with calamities and sufferings deserved or undeserved (for instance, Legge, 528). This Heaven, however, is thus subject to human manipulations for it can respond to sacrifices and supplications. The mature theology of *tian* found expression in the Han Confucian minister, Dong Zhongshu 董仲舒 and his many statements: for example, "Now Heaven is the ancestor of the myriad things, for the myriad things would not exist without Heaven 天者，萬物之祖。萬物非天不生"; "Now Heaven and Earth are the origin of myriad things, the source from which our deceased ancestors emerged 天地者，萬物之本，先祖之所出也"; "One can make life [i.e., to give birth to someone] but one cannot create a human, for that which creates a human is Heaven. A human *qua* human originates from Heaven, for Heaven is also the great grandfather of humans 為生不能為人，為人者天也。人之《為》人本于天，天亦人之曾祖父也." See his *Chunqiu fanlu* 春秋繁露 (*SBBY*) ch. 70 in 15: 5a; ch.33 in 9: 3a; ch. 41 in 11: 1a.

17. See *Zhuangzi jie* 莊子解, annotated by Wang Fuzhi 王夫之 (Beijing: Zhonghua, 1964), p. 48; pp. 115–16; and p. 278.

18. Oguchi and Hori, *ibid.*, p. 255.

19. Seng You 僧祐, comp., *Hongmingji* 弘明集 10: 3b (*SBCK* edition); the emperor's request is printed in 10: 1a–b, while Fayun's letter to the ministers in 1b–2a. These writings are also included in the *Quan Liangwen* 全梁文. For a brief account of Fan Zhen's attack and pro-Buddhist rebuttal in Wudi's court, see Kenneth Ch'en, *Buddhism in China: A Historical Survey* (Princeton: Princeton University Press, 1964), pp. 140–42.

20. In *Siku*, Jibu 集部, Biejilei 別集類: "Ruiyunsi ji 瑞雲寺記," in *Zetang ji* 則堂集 2.

21. See "Xiangmo bianwen," in *Dunhuang bianwen* 敦煌變文, ed. Wang Zhongmin 王重民 (2 vols. Beijing: Zhonghua, 1957; rpt. Taibei: Shijie shuju, 1977), 1: 361–62.

22. See Daoyuan 道原, *Jingde chuandeng lu* 景德傳燈錄 (*SBCK*. 30 *juan*. Shanghai: The Commcercial Press, 1935), 13:17b.

23. In *Siku*, Zibu 子部, Shijialei 釋家類.

24. For a lengthier discussion of the whole issue of the study of religion as first and foremost a discursive and, therefore, a linguistic affair, especially in regard to Chinese religion(s), see the brilliant essay by Robert Ford Campany, "On the Very Idea of Religions (in the Modern West and in Early Medieval China)," *History of Religions* 42/4 (May 2003): 287–319.

25. See Morohashi 5: 502 with *HDC* 5: 445.

26. *Mencius* 3A 3. Chinese text taken from the bi-lingual text of *Mencius*, trans. D. C. Lau (2 vols. Hong Kong: The Chinese University Press, 1984), 1: 98.

27. "Wangzhi [Royal Regulations] 王制," in *Liji zhuzi suoyin* 禮記逐字索引, eds. D. C. Lau and Chen Fong Ching (Hong Kong: The Commercial Press, 1992), p. 33.

28. *Shuowen jiezi* 說文解字, annotated by Duan Yucai 段玉裁 (fasc. rpt. of 1815 text. Taibei: Hanjing, 1984), 3b. 41a, p. 127. Emulation (*xiao* 教) in Xu's definition is, of course, another homophone of *xiao* 校, to teach, to rectify, in the Mencian remark.

29. *Songben Guangyun* 宋本廣韻 (4 vols., fasc. rpt. of 1705 text. Beijing: Laixunge, 1934), 4: 39a.

30. For disputed matters of authorship and text, see *Early Chinese Texts: A Bibliographical Guide*, ed. Michael Loewe (University of

California, Berkeley: The Society for the Study of Early China and The Institute of East Asian Studies, 1993), pp. 347–56. The text is frequently titled, *Comprehensive Discussion of Virtue in The White Tiger Hall* 白虎通德論.

31. *Baohu tongde lun* (*SBCK* ; fasc. rpt. of 1304 text. Shanghai: The Commercial Press, 1929), 7: 57.

32. For a counter example, see Campany, "On the Very Idea of Religions," p. 303.

33. *Ibid.*, pp. 308–09.

34. See Li Yanshou 李延壽, *Beishi* 北史, 33.

35. *Liji*, p. 60. For a modern account of how life's meaning and obligations are measured by the persistence of the ancestors, see the classic study by Francis L.K. Hsu, *Under the Ancestors' Shadow: Chinese Culture and Personality* (New York: Columbia University Press, 1948).

36. *Liji*, p. 126.

37. See Han Yu 韓愈, "Yuan Dao 原道," in *QTW* 全唐文 (5 vols. Shanghai: Guji chubanshe, 1990), 3: 2502—" 古之教者處其一，今之教者處其三."

38. Henry George Liddell and Robert Scott, *A Greek-English Lexicon*, with a revised supplement 1996 (Ninth ed. Oxford: Clarendon Press, 1940), p. 806.

39. Oguchi and Hori, p. 256; for the second reading, see Liu Cunren (Ts'un-yan) 柳存仁, *Daojiao shi tanyuan* 道教史探源 (Beijing: Beijing Daxue chubanshe, 2000), pp. 3–4.

40. Jonathan Z. Smith, *Imagining Religion: From Babylon to Jonestown* (Chicago: The University of Chicago Press, 1982), pp. 38–39.

41. It is gratifying to notice that, with the gradual political liberalization of China—at least in certain academic areas—the study of religion as an intellectual discipline is taken up again with renewed zest and expanded learning. Not only are Chinese savants adding many titles in recent years to an ever-lengthening list of publications on virtually all aspects of Chinese religions traditional and modern, elite and popular, but some of the publications are undertaking serious reckonings with Chinese religions fully informed by the discursive tradition forged by the "science of religion" or *Religionwissenschaft* of

the West and of Japan. Chinese scholars of religion, in other words, are no longer satisfied with merely regarding their subject matter as a part of *Hanxue* or Sinology, because they increasingly realize that, in method and understanding, any adequate account of a Chinese religion *qua* religion may involve reflection and research that transcend national, cultural, and linguistic boundaries. For a systematic and stimulating account of an emergent "science of religion" with Chinese accents and concerns by several hands, see Lü Daji 呂大吉, ed., *Zongjiaoxue tonglun* 宗教學通論 (rev. ed. of 1989 Beijing edition. Taibei: Boyuan chuban gongsi, 1993). See also Lai Chi-Tim [Li Zhitian] 黎志添, *Zongjiao yanjiu yu quanshixue: zongjiaoxue jianli di sikao* 宗教研究與詮釋學: 宗教學建立的思考 (Hong Kong: Chinese University of Hong Kong Press, 2003).

NOTES TO CHAPTER 3

1. For a more detailed development of this argument, see my "Enduring Change: Confucianism and the Prospect of Human Rights," *Lingnan Journal of Chinese Studies*, New Series, 2 (October 2000): 27–70. Slightly revised and without citations of Chinese script, the essay is reprinted in *Human Rights Review* 3/3 (April–June, 2002): 65–99.

2. See Joseph M. Kitagawa, *Religions of the East* (Philadelphia: Westminster Press, 1960).

3. See Lei Congyun, "Neolithic Sites of Religious Signifance," in Jessica Rawson, ed., *Mysteries of Ancient China: New Discoveries from the Early Dynasties* (New York: George Braziller, 1996), pp. 219–224. The earliest date concerns the so-called Upper Cave Man or more commonly known as the Peking Man. Cf. also Kwang-chih Chang, *Archeology of Ancient China*, 4th ed. rev. and enl. (New Haven: Yale University Press, 1986), pp. 61 ff. on possible evidence of "funeral rites" associated with the materials discovered; _____, "China on the Eve of the Historical Period," and Roger Bagley, "Shang Archeology," as respective Chapters 1 and 3 in *CHAC*, pp. 37–73; 124–231. See also L. Binford and C.K. Ho, "Taphonomy at a Distance: Zhoukoudian, 'The Cave Home of Bejing Man'?" in *Current Anthropology*

26 (1985): 413–442; L. Binford and N.M. Stone, "Zhoukoudian: A Closer Look," *Current Anthropology* 27/5 (1986): 453–475. I thank Professor David N. Keightley for the last two references.

4. An illuminating account may be found in David N. Keightley, "Clean Hands and Shining Helmets: Heroic Action in Early Chinese and Greek Culture," in *Religion and the Authority of the Past*, ed. Tobin Siebers (Ann Arbor: University of Michicagn Press, 1993), pp. 13–51.

5. Walter Burkert, *Greek Religion*, trans. John Raffan (Cambridge, Massachusetts: Harvard University Press, 1985), pp. 79–80; 190–99.

6. Gregory Nagy, *The Best of the Achaeans: Concepts of the Hero in Archaic Greek Poetry* (Baltimore: Johns Hopkins University Press, 1979), pp. 67–210. The classic study of the topic remains Erwin Rohde, *Psyche: Seelencult und Unsterblichkeitsglaube der Griechen* (2 vols., 8th ed. Tübingen: Mohr/Siebeck, 1910), Eng. trans. W.B. Hillis (New York: Harcourt, Brace, 1925).

7. Keightley, "Clean Hands," p. 19.

8. David N. Keightley, "The Shang: China's First Historical Dynasty," in *CHAC*, p. 251.

9. See Keightley, *ibid.*, p. 252 and footnote 36 for brief discussion and bibliography of relevant scholarship on the meaning of *di*. For the most recent dissent to the theory that this Shang figure might refer to an ancestor, see Michael Puett, *To Become a God: Cosmology, Sacrifice, and Self-Divinization in Early China* (Cambridge: Harvard University Asia Center for the Harvard-Yenching Institute, 2002), pp. 48–49.

10. For a succinct treatment, see Irene Eber, "The Interminable Term Question," *Bible in Modern China: The Literary and Intellectual Impact*, eds. Irene Eber, *et al.* Monumenta Serica Monograph Series XLIII (Sankt Augustin: Institute Monumenta Serica in cooperation with The Harry S. Truman Research Institute for the Advancement of Peace, The Hebrew University of Jerusalem, 1999), pp. 135–161. For more recent discussion of the subject, see the monumental study by Norman J. Girardot, *The Victorian Translation of China: James Legge's Oriental Pilgrimage* (Berkeley: University of California Press, 2002), pp. 276–285 and *passim*.

11. For the articulated debate and justification of adopting this imperial title by the Qin Emperor and his ministers, see *Shiji* 6; for an English translation of the account, see Sima Qian, *Records of The Grand Historian*, trans. Burton Watson, A *Renditions*—Columbia University Press Book (Hong Kong: Chinese University of Hong Kong, 1993), pp. 42–43. The more recent translation of the *Shiji* renders *huangdi* 皇帝 as "the majestic deified one." See William H. Nienhauser, ed. *The Grand Scribe's Records by Ssu-ma Ch'ien*, trans. Tsai-fa Cheng, et al., (Vol. 1, Bloomington: Indiana University Press, 1994), pp. 136. Chen Mengjia 陳夢家, in his celebrated classic study on divinatory inscriptions of the Shang period, has famously declared that "*Shangdi* or *di* not only executed his commands in the human world, but he also possessed his own court with messengers and subjects and the like to serve him . . . ." These subjects would include among them the ancestors of the human royal house. See *Yinxu buci zongshu* 殷虚卜辭綜述 (Beijing: Kexue chubanshe, 1956), p. 572.

12. See Chen, *ibid.*, chs. 16 and 17; also Li Minzhu 李民主, ed., *Yin-Shang shehui shenghuo shi* 殷商社会生活史 (Kaifeng: Henan renmin chubanshe, 1993), ch. 4.

13. David Keightley, "Theology and the Writing of History: Truth and the Ancestors in the Wu Ding Divination Records," *Journal of East Asian Archeology* 1/1–4 (1999): 208.

14. For Ricci's distinction between the love of parents and kin and the love of God, see his *The True Meaning of The Lord of Heaven*, pp. 384–85.

15. For the most thorough study of this aspect of ancestor worship, see Keightley, "The Making of the Ancestors: Late Shang Religion and Its Legacy," in *Religion and Chinese Society, Vol. I: Ancient and Medieval China*, ed. John Lagerwey (Hong Kong: The Chinese University and École française d'Extrême-Orient, 2004, I, 3–63).

16. See David M. Knipe, "*Sapiṇḍīkaraṇa*: The Hindu Rite of Entry into Heaven," in *Religious Encounters with Death: Insights from the History and Anthropology of Religions*, eds. Frank E. Reynolds and Earle H. Waugh (University Park: Pennsylvania State University Press, 1977), pp. 111–124. For an example of African practices, see

Benjamin Ray, "Death, Kingship, and Royal Ancestors in Buganda," in *ibid.*, pp. 56–70.

17. Keightley, in *CHAC*, pp. 254–55.

18. Jessica Rawson, "Western Zhou Archeology," in *CHAC*, p. 375.

19. *Ibid.*, pp. 428–430, 386.

20. Mark Lewis, "Warring States Political History," in *CHAC*, pp. 649–650.

21. Wu Hung, "Art and Architecture of the Warring States Period," in *CHAC*, p. 708.

22. For the importance of ancestor worship as a force of integration in Chinese social and familial life, see C.K. Yang, *op. cit.*, pp. 28–57; Francis L.K. Hsü, *Under the Ancestors' Shadow* (New York: Columbia University Press, 1948).

23. See Daniel L. Overmyer's magnificently detailed study in "Attitudes Toward Popular Religion in Ritual Texts of the Chinese State: *The Collected Statutes of the Great Ming,*" *Cahiers d'Extrême-Asie* 5 (1989–90): 191–221; the citation here is from p. 192.

24. The observation by E. Bruce Brooks and A. Taeko Brooks in *The Original Analects: Sayings of Confucius and His Successors* (New York: Columbia University Press, 1998), p. 114, that "the 'spirit' in 2:24 is ancestral" is well supported by the historical commentaries (Zhu Xi's, among others) based on the understanding reflected in a passage like *Zuo Commentary*, Duke Xi, Yr. 31: "Spirits not of one's kindred line [*zulei*] would not accept sacrifices." The assumption throughout much of the glosses on this passage of the *Analects* is that "spirits [*gui*]" here refers to one's natural or blood ancestors.

25. See the sections on "The Offices of Spring, [Domain of] the Clansman Earls 春官宗伯" in *Zhouli Zhengzhu* 周禮鄭注, 17–27 (*SBBY* edition). Offices, rituals, and deities described therein ostensibly trace their origin back to the time of the early Zhou, but modern scholarship dates this treatise as a likely Han document. See William G. Boltz, "Chou Li 周禮," in *Early Chinese Texts: A Bibliographical Guide*, ed. Michael Loewe (Berkeley: Society for the Study of Early China and The Institute of East Asian Studies, University of California, 1993), pp. 24–32; Michael Nylan, *The Five "Confucian" Classics* (New Haven:

Yale University Press, 2001), pp. 182–84. Concerning the hierarchical structure of this "pantheon" originating from the Shang-Zhou periods, different Chinese scholars have offered different interpretations. For the claim that the *di* of Shang religion was revered as the supreme deity and also a deified ancestor, see Guo Moruo 郭沫若, "Xian Qin tiandao guan zhi jinzhan 先秦天道观之进展," in *Qingtong shidai* 青铜时代 (Beijing: Kexue chubanshe, 1962). Hou Wailu 侯外庐, on the other hand, argues that this essentially theistic monism distinguishing Shang ancestor worship would give way to a "dualistic form of worship 二元崇拜" of the Zhou that included both gods and divine ancestors. See his *Zhongguo sixiang tongshi* 中国思想通史 (Beijing: Renmin chubanshe, 1980), pp. 63, 78. For the opposite view that the distinct worship of such a form of theistic dualism existed already in both Shang and Zhou, see Ren Jiyu 任继愈, ed., *Zhongguo zhexue fazhan shi* 中国哲学发展史 (Xian Qin juan 先秦卷) (Beijing: Renmin chubanshe, 1983), p. 83; Wang Yousan 王友三, ed., *Zhongguo zongjiao shi* 中国宗教史 (Jinan: Qilu shushe, 1991), p. 186.

26. *The HarperCollins Dictionary of Religion*, eds. Jonathan Z. Smith and William Scott Green, with The American Academy of Religion (New York: HarperCollins, 1995), p. 1086.

27. See Rudolf Otto, *Das Heilige: über das Irrationale in der Idee des Göttlichen und sein Verhältnis zum Rationalen* (Gotha: F.A. Perthes, 1924); English edition: *The Idea of the Holy: An Inquiry into the Non-rational Factor in the Idea of the Divine and its Relation to the Rational*, trans. John W. (London: Oxford University Press, 1952); _____, *Aufsätze das Numinose betreffend*, 2 vols., I , *Das ganz Andere* [The Wholly Other], and II, *Sünde und Urschuld* [Sin and Primal Guilt] (Gotha: L. Klotz, 1929).

28. For instance, Isaiah 55: 7–8. "For my thoughts are not your thoughts, neither are your ways my ways, says the Lord. For as the heavens are higher than the earth, so are my ways higher than your ways, and my thoughts than your thoughts" (quotation cited from the Revised Standard Version).

29. Jonathan Z. Smith, *Drudgery Divine: On the Comparison of Early Christianties and the Religions of Late Antiquity* (Chicago: University of Chicago Press, 1990), pp. 51, 52. See also his 1971 essay,

"*Adde Parvum Parvo Magnus Acervus Erit*," collected in *Map Is Not Territory: Studies in the History of Religions* (Leiden: E.J. Brill, 1978; rpt. Chicago: University of Chicago Press, 1993), pp. 240–264.

30. See Rey Chow, "Introduction: On Chineseness as a Theoretical Problem," in *Modern Chinese Literary and Cultural Studies in an Age of Theory: Reimagining a Field* (Durham, NC: Duke University Press, 2000), p. 10: ". . . the assertion of the Chinese difference tends often to operate from a set of binary oppositions in which the Western literary tradition is understood to be metaphorical, figurative, thematically concerned with transcendence, and referring to a realm that is beyond the world, whereas the Chinese literary tradition is said to metonymic, literal, immanentist, and self-referential (with literary signs referring not to an otherworldly realm above but back to the cosmic order of which the literary universe is part). The effort to promote China, in other words, is made through an a priori surrender to Western perspectives and categories."

31. See his *Offerings of Jade and Silk: Ritual and Symbol in the Legitimation of the T'ang Dynasty* (New Haven: Yale University Press, 1985), p. 123.

32. *Ibid.*, p. 125. For a fine discussion of ancestor worship and Tang politics, see pp. 126–141.

33. For a brief but excellent discussion, see Angela Zito, *Of Body and Brush: Grand Sacrifice as Text/Performance in Eighteenth-Century China* (Chicago: University of Chicago Press, 1997), pp. 127–130. According to Zito (pp. 127–28), "contention revolved around three interrelated problems: first, should Heaven and Earth be worshipped jointly in one ceremony or separately as they were in the eighteenth century; second, should this worship take place on open altars or in a temple; third, how many and which imperial ancestors should appear beside Heaven's spirit table as associative deities. At stake was the question of how literally the emperor's title of 'Son of Heaven' was to be taken. How closely was this man to be identified with a deity, and more important, how closely was his family's right to rule to be identified with the Mandate of Heaven?"

34. *Liji*, 11.20, p. 71.

35. *Offerings of Jade and Silk*, pp. 125–26.

36. I take the term from both the title and the content of the book by Zhang Rongming 張荣明, *Quanli di huangyan: Zhongguo chuantong di zhengzhi zongjiao* 权力的谎言—中国传统的政治宗教 (Hangzhou: Zhejiang renmin chubanshe, 2000).

37. See Joseph Chan, "A Confucian Perspective on Human Rights for Contemporary China," in *The East Asian Challenge for Human Rights*, eds., Joanne R. Bauer and Daniel A. Bell (New York: Cambridge University Press, 1999), pp. 235–36.

38. Allen J. Chun has argued in "Conceptions of Kingship and Kingship in Classical Chou China," *Toung Pao* 76 (1990): 16–48, that it was the priority of kingship that led to the ancient Chinese tendency to structure the family as a mini-state.

39. Fan Wenlan 范文瀾, *Zhongguo tongshi jianbian* 中國通史簡編, Vol. 1, rev. ed. (Beijing: Renmin chubanshe, 1949), pp. 38–39.

40. See my detailed discussion in "Enduring Change," esp. pp. 41–47. Cf. also Fan Wenlan, *op. cit.*, p. 205: "在儒家看來，提倡孝悌，在於防止犯上作亂，不問那個「犯」和「亂」是否合理."

41. For a brief discussion of the problem of the private (*si* 私) in politics and ethics, see my *Rereading the Stone: Desire and the Making of Fiction* (Princeton: Princeton University Press, 1997), pp. 176–79; and "The Real Tripitaka Revisited: International Religion and National Politics," *ASIANetwork Exchange* Viii/2 (Winter 2000), 13, and note 14.

42. D.W.Y. Kwok, "In the Rites and Rights of Being Human," in Wm. Theodore de Bary and Tu Weiming, eds., *Confucianism and Human Rights* (New York: Columbia University Press, 1998), p. 85.

43. Confucius's judgment is echoed and expanded upon by his disciple Zeng Shen 曾參 allegedly in *The Great Learning*: "The gentleman, without going beyond his household, is able to perfect his teachings for the state 故君子不出家，而成教於國." See *The Great Learning*, in Legge, I: 370.

44. Chang I-jen 張以仁, William G. Bolz and Michael Loewe, "Kuo yü 國語," in *Early Chinese Texts: A Bibliographical Guide*, ed. Michael Loewe (Berkeley: The Society for the Study of Early China and The Institute of East Asian Studies, University of California, 1993), p. 263.

45. "Lu Yu shang 魯語上," in *Guoyu* 國語 4: 6a, 7a–b (*SBBY* edition).

46. The first pioneering study that gives a detailed sketch of the topic, tracing it from the time of the close of the Warring States down to the Republican Era, has to be the informative account by John K. Shryock cited in footnote 13 in Chapter 2 above. My rehearsal of the topic here is necessarily brief, and I gladly and gratefully acknowledge my dependence on Shryock and on the more recent and munificent scholarship of Dr. Huang Chin-hsing [Huang Jinxing] 黄進興. See his *You ru shengyu: quanli, xinyang yu zhengdang xing* 優入聖域: 權力，信仰與正當性 (Taibei: Yunchen wenhua chubanshe, 1994), and "The Confucian Temple as a Ritual System: Manifestations of Power, Belief and Legitimacy in Traditional China," *The Tsing Hwa Journal of Chinese Studies*, New Series 25/2 (June 1995): 115–136. A recent essay in English breaks further ground by bringing a comparative perspective to bear (in relationship to Hinduism in this case) on the subject of sacrifice. See Thomas A. Wilson, "Sacrifice and the Imperial Cult of Confucius," *History of Religions* 41/3 (Febrary 2002): 251–287, and still more recently, the splendid volume edited by him: *On Sacred Grounds: Culture, Society, Politics, and the Formation of the Cult of Confucius* (Cambridge, Massachusetts: Harvard University Asia Center, 2002). Wilson's writings that focus on the details of the ritual sacrifices to Confucius and their sporadic modifications nicely complement Huang's attention to the physical, architectural, and symbolic aspects of the shrine. A minor criticism of Wilson may be voiced in his questionable choice of Henry Hubert and Marcel Mauss's *Sacrifice: Its Nature and Functions* for almost the sole theoretical ballast of his study, since that book's heavy emphasis on sacrifice as an act of expiation obscures other important functions of sacrifice that may not involve notions of sin and guilt.

47. *Chunqiu Zuozhuan jinzhu jinyi* 春秋左傳今註今譯, annotated and trans., Li Zongtong 李宗桐 (3 vols. Taibei: Commercial Press, 1971), *juan* 30; 3: 1484. The name and the Duke's elegiac tribute are recorded again in *Liji*, p. 21 ("Tangong," 3: 107). Commentators have glossed "father/sire (*fu* 父)" with *fu* 甫, a euphemism for either a handsome father or a handsome man. Subsequent literary references to Ni Fu, however, always point only to Confucius: for example, Chenggong Zi'an, "Rhapsody on Whistling," ll. 139–140, in *Wen Xuan or Selec-*

tions of Refined Literature, trans. and annotated David R. Knechtges (Vol. 3. Princeton: Princeton University Press, 1996), p. 323.

48. Ban Gu 班固, *Hanshu* 漢書 (12 vols. Hong Kong: Zhonghua shuju, 1970), *juan 67*; 9: 2924–25.

49. For the various titles often based on allusions to the earliest Confucian documents like the *Analects* and *Mencius* that were deployed to constitute Confucius as the paragon Sage and Teacher of all times, see Wilson, "Sacrifice," 266–68.

50. *Hanshu*, 9: 2926–27.

51. "The Confucian Temple," 119.

52. Wilson, "Sacrifices," 258, 284.

53. Huang, "The Confucian Temple," *loc. cit.*

54. *Ibid.*, 127–28.

55. *Ibid.*, 123.

56. Thomas H. C. Lee, *Education in Traditional China: A History* (Leiden: Brill, 2000), p. 75, emphasis added; see also the entire chs. 2 and 3 for Lee's magisterial account of both the institutional and intellectual history of traditional Chinese education.

57. Wilson, "Sacrifice," 262, 263.

58. *Kongfu dang'an xuanbian* 孔府檔案選編 (Beijing: Zhonghua shuju, 1982), 1:17, cited in Huang, "The Confucian Temple," 120.

59. *Ibid.*, 126.

60. Wilson, "Sacrifice," 269.

61. Kong Jifen,孔繼汾, *Queli wenxian kao* 闕里文獻考 (1753), 11:1a, cited in Huang, *Youru*, p. 165. See pp. 166–68 for further discussion and evidence of the Qing emperors's regard for honoring Confucius through state ritual.

62. Huang, "The Confucian Temple," 133.

NOTES TO CHAPTER 4

1. For a thorough analysis of ritual and desire in Xunzi, see my *Rereading the Stone*, Chapter 2.

2. Ma Xisha 马西沙, "Preface 序言," in Ma Xisha and Han Bing-fang 韩秉方, *Zhongguo minjian zongjiaoshi* 中国民间宗教史 (Shanghai: Renmin chubanshe, 1992), p. 1.

3. Kristofer Schipper, *The Taoist Body*, trans. Karen C. Duval (Berkeley: University of California Press, 1993), p. 9.

4. Barbara Hendrischke, "Earlier Daoist Movements," in *Daoism Handbook*, ed. Livia Kohn (Leiden: Brill, 2000), p. 140.

5. The last graph *xie* in the last term is itself another significant term, since it is the classic antonym to the concept of *zheng* 正 and all its venerable connotations of uprightness, rectitude, straightness, and orthodoxy. *Xie*, glossed by the *Shuowen* as "bu zheng," thus takes the opposite meanings of perversity, deviancy, slantedness, and heresy. The word's contemporary currency is only too familiar when a movement like Falun Gong was branded by the state as a *xie jiao*.

6. Chen Shou, *Sanguo zhi* 三國志 (5 vols. Beijing: Zhonghua shuju, 1959), *juan* 8, 1: 264.

7. See *Zuo Commentary*, Duke Cheng 13: "國之大事，在祀與戎."

8. "Yu-Xia shu, Yao dian 虞夏書，堯典," in *Shangshu jishi* 尚書集釋, annotated and ed., Qu Wanli 屈萬里 (Taibei: Lianjing, 1983), p. 18. Commentators have various explanations for the "Six Honored Ones (六宗)," including the sun, the moon, the stars in the sky, Mount Tai, the Yellow River, and the sea on earth.

9. "Chu Yu xia 楚語下," in *Guoyu* 18: 3b.

10. For the succinct statement of this all too familiar topic, see Michel Foucault, "The Discourse on Language," Appendix in *The Archeology of Knowledge and The Discourse on Language*, trans. A.M. Sheridan Smith (New York: Pantheon, 1972), pp. 215–238. The precursors to his own thinking named by Foucault include Gaston Bachelard, Georges Canguilhem, Georges Dumézil, and Jean Hyppolite.

11. See Nathan Sivin, "State, Cosmos, and Body in the Last Three Centuries B.C.," *Harvard Journal of Asiatic Studies* 55/1 (June 1995): 5–38, and more recently, Geoffrey Lloyd and Nathan Sivin, *The Way and the Word: Science and Medicine in Early China and Greece* (New Haven: Yale University Press, 2002), pp. 194–238. The correlation between rulership and omens manifestly has very ancient roots and the notion studs many classical texts. One proverbial saying frequently cited even today comes from *Doctrine of the Mean* 中庸 24: "When a nation or a family is about to flourish, there are sure to be auspicious signs; but when a nation or a family is about to perish,

there will certainly be bogies and accursed beings 妖孽 [in manife-station]."

12. See Wolfram Eberhard, "Beiträge zum kosmologischen Spe-kulation Chinas in der Han Zeit," *Bressler Archiv* 16 (Berlin: Museum für Völkerkunde, 1933): 1–100; _____, "Index zu den Arbeiten über Astronomie, Astrologie, und Elementlehre," *Monumenta Sinica* 7 (1932): 242–66; _____, "The Political Function of Astronomy and Astrology in Han China," in *Chinese Thought and Institutions*, ed. John K. Fairbank (Chicago: University of Chicago Press, 1957), pp. 33–70; and *Sternkunde und Weltbild im alten China* (Taipei: Chinese Materials and Research Aids Service Center, 1970). For Zheng Zhim-ing, see 鄭志明, *Zhongguo shehui yu zongjiao* 中國社會與宗教 (Taibei: Xuesheng shudian, 1986). That the so-called "correlative cosmology" generally labeled as a Han invention has earlier roots may be seen in a text like the *Xinyu* 新語 attributed to Lu Jia 陸賈 (*ca. 228–ca.* 140 B.C.E.). See B: 7b: "Therefore, when the world declines and the Way perishes, these are not what Heaven has accomplished, but what a ruler of the state has elected to bring to pass . . . . When the Way is lost in the realm below, then the Heavenly patterns above would fittingly measure such a situation. When wicked government spread among the people, then insects and calamities would arise on earth 故 世衰道亡，非天之所為也，乃國君有所取之也 . . . . 道失於下，則天文 度於上；惡政流於民，則蟲災生於地" (*SBBY* edition).

13. *Ibid.*, pp. 85–112.

14. Aihe Wang, *Cosmology and Political Culture in Early China* (Cambridge: Cambridge University Press, 2000), p. 174. The term *jingcheng* can be found in *Huananzi* 20: 1b. "Thus essential sincerity will be felt within, and formative pneuma will move in the heavens 故 精誠感於內，形氣動於天" (*SBBY* edition). According to the lexicons, the term is fairly common to Han and post-Han texts of different ideological affiliations. However its meaning is to be construed in the *Huananzi*, it is interesting to notice that by the Tang, Bai Juyi 白居 易 in his poetic fictionalization of the romance between the emperor Xuanzong and Yang Guifei associated it explicitly with Daoist ritual. See the famous "Changhen ge 長恨歌," in *Bai Xiangshan shiji* 白香山 詩集 12: 8b. "臨邛道士鴻都客，能以精誠致魂魄" (*SBBY* edition).

15. Aihe Wang, p. 206. For further discussion of recent scholarship on the subject of "correlative cosmology," see her excellent critical survey, ""Correlative Cosmology: From the Structure of Mind to Embodied Practice," in *Bulletin of The Museum of Far Eastern Antiquities* 72 (Stockholm 2000): 110–132. The entire special issue is devoted to "Reconsidering the Correlative Cosmology of Early China."

16. See Robert Ford Campany, *Strange Writing: Anomaly Accounts in Early Medieval China* (Albany: State University of New York Press, 1996), p. 102. Campany's book provides the most thorough and authoritative study of the genre of writings and related topics to date.

17. *Ibid.*, pp. 274, 277.

18. For an illuminating treatment of the Tang court's treatment of omens, see Wechsler, *Offerings*, ch. 3.

19. *Shiji* 6, 1: 237–38.

20. *Ibid.*, 28, 4: 1468.

21. *Ibid.*, 4: 1370.

22. *Ibid.*, 6, 1: 247.

23. *Ibid.*, 1: 263, 259.

24. *Ibid.*, 1: 252. Later, the Han commentator Zheng Xuan, with perfect hindsight, wrote that Hu here obviously meant Hu Hai, the heir who succeeded the emperor and soon lost the empire.

25. *Ibid.*, 1: 257.

26. *Ibid.*, 1: 264.

27. *Ibid.*, 1: 258.

28. *Ibid.*, 1: 282.

29. *Ibid.*, 1: 283.

30. On how different groups of religious rebels in the Latter Han called themselves "the perfected ones," see Kohn, *Daoism Handbook*, pp. 137, 153. On *fangshi*, see Ngo Van Xuyet, *Divination, magie et politiques dans la Chine ancienne* (Paris: Presses Universitaires de France, 1976); Kenneth DeWoskin, *Doctors, Diviners and Magicians of Ancient China: Biographies of Fang-shih* (New York: Columbia University Press, 1981).

31. *Shiji* 28, 4: 1378.

32. *Ibid.*, 4: 1381.

33. *Ibid.*, 4: 1384.

34. *Ibid.*, 4: 1404.

35. *Ibid.*, 4: 1385.

36. *Ibid.*, 4: 1386.

37. For a convenient and informative account, see Michael Loewe's chapter on "The Former Han Dynasty," especially the section aptly titled "The full force of modernist policies (141–87 B.C.)," in *CHC*, pp. 152–178.

38. *Hanshu* 56, 8: 2495–96.

39. *Ibid.*, 8: 2523.

40. For informative discussions, see Wei Zhengtong 韋政通, *Dong Zhongshu* 董仲舒 (Taibei: Dongda tushu, 1986), pp. 185–213; Lü Xichen 吕锡琛, *Daojia, Fangshi yu wangchao zhengzhi* 道家方士与王朝政治 (Changsha: Hunan chubanshe, 1991), pp. 96–108.

41. Loewe, "The Former Han Dynasty," p. 171.

42. *Ibid.*, pp. 207–210.

43. For further elaboration of how early Daoist philosophical discourse disputes Confucian teachings, see my "Reading The *Daodejing*: Ethics and Politics of the Rhetoric," in *Chinese Literature: Essays, Articles, Reviews* 25 (2003): 169–191.

44. Stephan Feuchtwang, *Popular Religion in China: The Imperial Metaphor* (Richmond: 2001), pp. 43–44.

45. Ge Hong, *Baopuzi* 抱朴子 18: 12a–b (*SBBY* edition). For discussions of doctrinal developments relative to imagistic and physio-biological utilization of the body, see Schipper, *op. cit.*, esp. chs. 6 and 7; Catherine Despeux, *Taoïsme et corps humaine: le "Xiuzhen Tu"* (Paris: Editions de la Maisnie, 1994).

46. See Cao Zhi 曹植," Bian Dao lun 辯道論," in *QQHS* 2: 1151–52.

47. See *Jinshu* 晉書, *juan* 8, "Ai Di ji 哀帝紀."

48. *Weishu* 魏書, *juan* 114, "Shi Lao zhi 釋老志."

49. For an interesting account, see Liu Jingcheng 劉精誠, *Zhongguo Daojiao shi* 中國道教史 (Taibei: Wenjin chubanshe, 1993), pp. 180–212.

50. See *ibid.*, pp. 130–163; Kohn, *Handbook*, pp. 274–77, 196–200, 284–85. See also Michel Strickmann, "On the Alchemy of T'ao Hung-ching," and Richard B. Mather, "K'ou Ch'ien-chih and the

Taoist Theocracy at the Northern Wei Court, 425–451," both in *Facets of Taoism: Essays in Chinese Religion,* eds. Holmes Welch and Anna Seidel (New Haven: Yale University Press, 1979), pp. 123–192 and 103–122.

51. The last term is memorably enshrined in a line of regulated verse by the famous Daoist scholar and sometime state official in the Song, Chen Tuan 陳摶 (?–989). In his poem "Departing from the Court 辭朝," the fifth line reads: "Grieved by hearing that swords and halberds are supporting a precarious lord 愁聞劍戟扶危主." See *Quan Song shi* 全宋詩 (72 Vols. Beijing: Beijing daxue chubanshe, 1991–98), 1: *juan* 1, 9. I thank my colleague David Roy for tracking down this reference for me.

52. Robert Bagley, "Shang Archeology," in *CHAC,* p. 230.

53. *Shiji* 121, 10:3122.

54. The phrase derives from the opening section of Emperor Wudi's edict inaugurating the dialogical discussion with his ministers cited in footnote 130: "If the Three Dynasties had received [the Heavenly] Mandate, where is the talismanic evidence 三代受命，其符安在?" Wudi's diction here may find numerous echoes in Han documents, among which Sima Qian's own summary of Zou Yan's teachings can serve as a potent example: "He claimed that ever since the definitive division of Heaven and Earth, the Five Powers have been changing in succession. When every aspect of governance is fitting, then talismanic correspondence would be similarly appropriate 稱引天地剖判以來，五德轉移，治各有宜，而符應若茲." See *Shiji* 74, 7: 2344.

55. The phrase is associated with the story of a certain Gan Zhong 甘忠 from the region of Qi in his attempt to gain favor with the Emperor Chengdi (32 BCE-6 CE). He allegedly "forged . . .12 *juan* of the *Classic of Great Peace of the Bao-Yuan,* so as to speak about 'how the Han household, about to encounter the great end of Heaven and Earth, should receive once more the Mandate from Heaven 詐做 . . . 包元太平經十二卷，以言漢家逢天地之大終，當更受命於天'." See *Hanshu* 75, 10: 3192.

56. Fan Ye 范曄, *Hou Hanshu* 後漢書101. A brief episode of Zhang's revolt was, of course, immortalized in the Ming novel, *Sanguo*

yanyi. For a more poetic rendering of the ditty, see *Three Kingdoms: A Historical Novel*, trans. Moss Roberts (Berkeley: University of California Press, and Beijing: Foreign Language Press, 1991), p. 6.

57. Among other documents, the most convenient Daoist source is the *Laojun yinsongjie jing* 老君音誦戒經, *DZ* 562. The secular source would be the *Jinshu* 晉書, 8, 106, 118. For scholarly discussions, see Anna K. Seidel, "The Image of the Early Ruler in Early Taoist Messianism: Lao-tzu and Li Hung," *History of Religions* 9/2 and 3 (November 1969–February 1970): 216–237; Tang Yongtong 湯用彤, *Tang Yongtong xueshu lunwen ji* 湯用彤学术论文集 (Beijing: Zhonghua shuju, 1983), pp. 309–311.

58. *Hou Hanshu* 7.

59. For a detailed treatment of Zhang Ling and Zhang Lu, see Qing Xitai 卿希泰, *et al.*, *Zhongguo Daojiao shi* 中国道教史 (rev. ed. 3 vols. Chengdu: Sochuan renmin chubanshe, 1996), 1: 101–253.

60. See *Sanguo zhi* 15 and 23.

61. See Qing, 1: 240.

62. *QQHS* 2: 1151.

63. See *Guang Hongmingji* 12; "Datong zhi 大同志," in *Huayang guozhi* 華陽國志 8.

64. See Qing Xitai, 1: 279; Liu Jingcheng, p. 89.

65. See "Biography of Zhang Chang 張昌傳," in *Jinshu* 100.

66. The extensive account of Li and family members is found in the *Jinshu*, 120–21.

67. Terry Kleeman, *Great Perfection: Religion and Ethnicity in a Chinese Millennial Kingdom* (Honolulu: University of Hawai'i Press, 1998), p. 107. Kleeman's monograph is the most thorough study of the Li regime in any language.

68. Contemporary scholarship devoted to the study of religious traditions and communities of historical China that fall outside of the three principal religions of Confucianism, Daoism, and Buddhism is enormous, particularly the part of which that treats later medieval and early modern periods not convered under the present study. From the selected bibliography immediately following, it can readily be seen that virtually all so-called "popular" or "local" religious traditions would—at one time or another, in one way or another—resist

or attempt to circumvent official governmental control. The result could range from mutual accommodation, through persistent simmering tension, to open conflict. A handy, comprehensive reference in Chinese is the previously cited text authored by Ma Xisha and colleagues, *Zhongguo minjian zongjiao shi*, and it is part of Ma's very thesis (p. 10) that "popular religions (*minjian zongjiao*)" are by definition those "religions that cannot fit into the feudal ruling order 不符合封建统治秩序." In the light of certain taxonomical verdicts by the PRC government currently, Ma's words seem especially audacious when he emphatically asserts on the same page: "Even 'deviant religions' are also religions '邪教'也是宗教." Other representative studies of different movements, communities, rituals, and figures spanning the Song to late imperial times in Western languages may include: Cynthia J. Brokaw, *The Ledgers of Merit and Demerit: Social Change and Moral Order in Late Imperial China* (Princeton: Princeton University Press, 1991); Roderick Cave, *Chinese Paper Offerings* (Hong Kong: Oxford University Press, 1998); Paul Cohen, *History in Three Keys: The Boxers as Event, Experience, and Myth* (New York: Columbia University Press, 1997); Edward L. Davis, *Society and the Supernatural in Song China* (Honolulu: University of Hawai'i Press, 2001); Kenneth Dean, *Lord of the Three in One: The Spread of a Cult in Southeast China* (Princeton: Princeton University Press, 1998); Lothar von Falkenhausen, "Archeology and the Study of Chinese Local Religion: A Discussant's Remarks," *Cahiers d'Extrême-Asie* 10 (1998): 411–425; Stephan Feuchtwang, "The Study of Chinese Popular Religion," *Revue Européenne des sciences sociales* 27/84 (1989): 69–86; Vincent Goossaert, *Dans les temples de la Chine. Histoire des cultes, vie des communautées* (Paris: Albin Michel, 2000); Valerie Hansen, *Changing Gods in Medieval China, 1127–1276* (Princeton: Princeton University Press, 1990); David Johnson, ed., *Ritual and Scripture in Chinese Popular Religion: Five Studies* (Berkeley: University of California Press, 1995); Paul Katz, *Demon Hordes and Burning Boats: The Cult of Marshal Wen in Late Imperial Chekiang* (Albany: State University of New York Press, 1995); Liu Kwang-Ching, ed., *Orthodoxy in Late Imperial China* (Berkeley: University of California Press, 1990); Kwang-Ching Liu and Richard Shek, eds., *Heterodoxy in Late Imperial China*

(Honolulu: University of Hawai'i Press, 2004); Joseph McDermott, ed., *State and Court Ritual in China* (Cambridge: Cambridge University Press, 1999); Susan Naquin, *Peking: Temples and City Life, 1400–1900* (Berkeley: University of California Press, 2000); _____ and Chün-fang Yu, eds., *Pilgrims and Sacred Sites in China* (Berkeley: University of California Press, 1992); Daniel Overmyer, *Folk Buddhist Religion: Dissenting Sects in Late Traditional China* (Cambridge, Massachusetts: Harvard University Press, 1976); _____, "Alternatives: Popular religious sects in Chinese society," *Modern China* 7/2 (1981): 153–190; _____, "Attitudes toward the Ruler and State in Chinese Popular Religious Literature: Sixteenth and Seventeenth Century *pao-chuan*," *HJAS* 44/2 (1984): 347–379; Meir Shahar and Robert Weller, eds., *Unruly Gods: Divinity and Society in China* (Honolulu: University of Hawai'i Press, 1996); Jonathan Spence, *God's Chinese Son: The Taiping Heavenly Kingdom of Hong Xiuquan* (New York: Norton, 1996); and B.J. Ter Haar, *The White Lotus Teachings in Chinese Religious History* (Leiden: Brill, 1992).

69. See Kohn, *Handbook*, pp. 352–53.

70. Campany, *Strange Writing*, pp. 118–19.

71. See Sima Guang 司馬光, *Zizhi tongjian* 資治通鑑 (10 vols. Beijing: Guji, 1956, based on printed edn. of 1139), 181–82; 6: 5636–5701.

72. See "Ritual 禮, Section 7," in *Song shi* 宋史 104, for a detailed description of the emperor's canonization of his ancestors and his parents as Daoist deities and the ceremonies connected with his reception of new revelations inscribed in Celestial Writings (*tianshu*).

NOTES TO CHAPTER 5

1. See Kenneth Ch'en, *Buddhism*, pp. 20–42; Ren Jiyu 任继愈, *Zhongguo fojiao shi* 中国佛教史 (Vol. 1. Beijing: Zhongguo shehui kexue chubanshe, 1981), p. 67.

2. The two words in quotation marks are convenient allusions to two familiar works of scholarship: E. Zürcher, *The Buddhist Conquest of China*, 2 vols. (Leiden: Brill, 1959), and Kenneth K.S. Ch'en, *The Chinese Transformation of Buddhism* (Princeton: Princeton University Press, 1973).

3. For the following sketch of Indian and Buddhism's general influence on Chinese culture and the later short section on Xuanzang, the scripture-pilgrim, I have adopted portions of my "The Real Tripitaka Revisited: International Religion and National Politics," *ASIANetwork Exchange* III/2 (Winter, 2000): 9–16.

4. See Hu Shi(h) 胡適, "Fojiao di fanyi wenxue 佛教的翻譯文學," in *Baihua wenxue shi* 白話文學史 (Taibei: Qiming, 1957), pp. 157–215. Hu's 1928 thesis (dating from his Preface) was re-opened, expanded, and debated in 1983 by contemporary colleagues in Chinese literature. See "Symposium: The Origin of Chinese Fiction [Essays by Victor H. Mair, Kenneth J. Dewoskin, and W. L. Idema]," in *CLEAR* 5/1–2 (July 1983): 1–52.

5. The estimation is based on vocabulary count in the *T*. See Liang Qichao, "Fanyi wenxue yu fodian 翻譯文學與佛典," in *Foxue yanjiu shiba pian* 佛學研究十八篇 (Taibei: Zhonghua, 1966, rpt. of 1936 edition), p. 27 (N.B. Page numbers refer to individual essays collected in the volume).

6. For Indian literary references and themes in Chinese writings, see *Zhong-Yin wenxue guanxi yuanliu* 中印文學关系源流, ed. Yu Longyu 郁龙余 (Changsha: Hunan wenyi chubanshe, 1987). On language, translation, literary, and linguistic issues, see Rao Zongyi 饒宗頤, *Zhong-Yin wenhua guanxishi lunji: yuwen pian* 中印文化關係史論集語文篇 (Hong Kong: Chinese University of Hong Kong, 1990); Victor H. Mair and Tsu-lin Mei, "The Sanskrit Origins of Recent Style Prosody," in *HJAS* 51/2 (December, 1991): 375–470; Victor H. Mair, "Buddhism and the Rise of the Written Vernacuclar in East Asia: The Making of National Languages," in *JAS* 53/3 (August, 1994): 707–751; and Helwig Schmidt-Glintzer and Victor H. Mair, "Buddhist Literature," in *The Columbia History of Chinese Literature*, ed. Victor H. Mair (New York: Columbia University Press, 2001), pp. 160–172.

7. See Victor H. Mair, *T'ang Transformation Texts* (Cambridge, Massachusetts: Council of East Asian Studies, Harvard University, 1989), and *Painting and Performance: Chinese Picture Recitation and Its Indian Genesis* (Honolulu: University of Hawaii Press, 1988).

8. For numerous transfers of both knowledge and materials from India to China—from astronomy and mathematics, through metal-

lurgy, printing, and medicine, to various agricultural techniques (for example, the method of crystallizing sugar)—one should consult the encyclopedic accounts in Joseph Needham's *Science and Civilisation in China*, 18 vols. For Buddhism's contribution to education in medieval China, see Erik Zürcher, "Buddhism and Education in T'ang Times," in *Neo-Confucian Education: The Formative Stage*, eds. William Theodore de Bary and John W. Chaffee (Berkeley: University of California Press, 1989), pp. 19–56, and Lee, *Education in Traditional China*, pp. 214–223, 269–276. For Indian influences of Chinese religious beliefs, practices, symbolisms, and institutions both within and beyond Buddhism, see Erik Zürcher, "Buddhist Influence on Early Taoism, A Survey of Scriptural Evidence," *T'oung Pao* LXVI/1–3 (1980): 84–148; Stephen Teiser, *The Ghost Festival in Medieval China* (Princeton: Princeton University Press, 1988); _____, *The Scripture on the Ten Kings and the Making of Purgatory in Medieval Chinese Buddhism* (Honolulu: University of Hawaii Press, 1994); Valerie Hansen, "Gods on Walls: A Case of Indian Influence on Chinese Lay Religion?" in *Religion and Society in T'ang and Sung China*, eds. Patricia Buckley Ebrey and Peter N. Gregory (Honolulu: University of Hawaii Press, 1993), pp. 75–114.

9. *Xiaojing zhushu* 孝經注疏 2,5 in *Shisanjing zhushu* 十三經注疏 (2 vols. fasc. rpt . of Qing edition critically ed. Ruan Yuan 阮元. Beijing: Zhonghua shuju, 1979), 2: 2548.

10. Text taken from Sun Chuo 孫綽, "Yu Dao lun 喻道論," in *Hongming ji* 3: 17b–18a.

11. See Monk Shunshi 順釋 of the Liang (502–56), "Sanpo lun 三破論," in *ibid.*, 8: 16a.

12. Daoxuan 道宣, " Xu liedai wangchen zhihuojie xia 敘列代王臣滯惑解下," in *Guang Hongmingji* 廣弘明集 7 in *T.* 52: 129. .

13. See, for example, the Monk Daoan 道安, in *Er jiao lun* 二教論, 23, "Section 12, Yifa chuyi 依法除疑," in *QQHS* 4: 4005: "However, when Buddhist teachings become even slightly prominent, they would vie with each other in their excesses. They would abolish the resources for parents above and destroy the proper shares of wives and children below 然釋訓稍陵，競為奢侈，上滅父母之資，下損妻孥之分."

14. Erik Zürcher has divided the many-sided critique ("anti-clericalism") mounted by official elites over several centuries of early Chinese Buddhism into four main types: political and economic arguments against the Buddhist detriment to the state's stability and prosperity; utilitarian arguments against the "non-productive" mode of monastic life; cultural superiority arguments against Buddhism's foreign origin and practices; and moral arguments against violations of "sacred canons of social behavior." See *op. cit.*, 1: 254–285.

15. See Teiser, *Ghost Festival*; for Zongmi, see Peter N. Gregory, *Tsung-mi and the Sinification of Buddhism* (Princeton: Princeton University Press, 1991). The Chinese critique of Buddhist ethics and the manner of Buddhist rebuttal has been well rehearsed by Kenneth Ch'en in *The Chinese Transformation*, pp. 14–64. Professor Ch'en, however, writes largely as someone taking a more-or-less neutral position between Buddhism and Confucianism. For someone like Sun Guangde, a convinced Confucian, the Buddhist counter-arguments are often dismissed as forced, illogical, and evasive. See *Jin Nan-Bei chao*, pp. 40–68.

16. "From a deeper level of observation, it will not be difficult for us to discover quite a few Buddhist Masters of the Northern Song who became not only the potent advocates of rebuilding human social order but also the meritorious contributors to the revival of Confucian learning 深一層的觀察，我們便不難發現，北宋不少佛教大師不但是重建人間秩序的有力推動者，而且也是儒學復興的功臣." This brief citation cannot do justice to the magisterial sweep and depth of erudition exemplified in the latest scholarship from Professor Yü Ying-shih(shi). See 余英時, *Zhu Xi di lishi shijie: Song dai shidafu zhengzhi wenhua di yanjiu* 朱熹的歷史世界：宋代士大夫政治文化的研究 (2 vols. Taibei: Yunchen congkan, 2003), 1: 116. The entire first part of this work and, indeed, much of the other sections of the two volume masterpiece are germane to many of the issues touched on in the present study.

17. *Sima shi shuyi* 司馬氏書儀, in Zhang Haipeng 張海鵬 (1755–1816), *Xuejin taoyuan* 學津討原 (100 *ce*. Shanghai: Hanfenlou fascm. ed., 1912–35), *ce* 31, 5: 8b–9a. See also Patricia Buckley Ebrey, "The Response of the Sung State to Popular Funeral Practices," in *Religion and Society in T'ang and Sung China*, eds. Patricia Buckley Ebrey

and Peter N. Gregory (Honolulu: Hawaii University Press, 1993), pp. 209–239 for further discussion of Sima's critique of other Buddhist beliefs and rites.

18. To quote a recent work of monumental scholarship, "the feminization of Kuan-yin and new developments in religious Taoism could be seen as responses to the patriarchal stance of institutional Buddhism and Neo-Confucianism. The latter, for practical purposes, was the state religion of late imperial China [as it was also for early imperial China]. If Neo-Confucianism and organized Buddhism had not lacked feminine symbols and female practicioners, Kuan-yin may not have undergone a sexual transformation. We can look at this together with the two factors I already mentioned. Namely, because China already possessed an ideology of kingship, Kuan-yin did not become connected with the royalty, as Avalokiteśvara did in other Asian countries. And because China did not have a native tradition of universal saviors, Kuan-yin could and did occupy the empty space with amazing success. One of the strengths of Buddhism, it seems to me, is that it always supplied what was lacking in the native traditions. That is why alone among all imported religions, Buddhism could have 'gone native' and become accepted as one of the Three Teachings of China." See Chün-fang Yü, *Kuan-yin: the Chinese Transformation of Avalokiteśvara* (New York: Columbia University Press, 2001), p. 21.

19. See the authoritative study by Daniel Overmyer, *Precious Volumes: An introduction Chinese Sectarian Scriptures form the Sixteenth and Seventeenth Centuries* (Cambridge: Harvard University Press, 1999).

20. See Rita Gross, *Buddhism After Patriarchy: A Feminist History, Analysis and Reconstruction of Buddhism* (Albany: State University of New York Press, 1993).

21. See Zhu Xi, "Quan nü Dao huansu bang 勸女道還俗榜," in *Huian xiansheng Zhu Wengong wenji* 晦庵先生朱文忠公文集 (Shanghai: Shangwu, 1929?, *SBCK* rpt. of Ming Jiajing ed.), 100 (in Case 7, ce 46).

22. I quote from a ground-breaking and lengthy essay by Zhou Yiqun, in "The Hearth and the Temple: Mapping Female Religiosity

in Late Imperial China, 1550–1900," *Late Imperial China* 24.2 (2003): 109–155.

23. "Chu Wang Ying zhuan 楚王英傳," in *Hou Hanshu*, 72.

24. For brief description of the beginning of what would become an accepted linguistic practice of long standing in Chinese Buddhism, see Erik Zürcher, *Buddhist Conquest*, 1: 39–40.

25. Liang Qichao, "Zhongguo fofa xingshuai yange shuolue 中國佛法興衰沿革說略," in *Foxue shiba pien*, pp. 2–3.

26. *Transformation of Buddhism*, p. 66.

27. Leon Hurvitz, "'Render Unto Caesar' in Early Chinese Buddism: Hui-yüan's Treatise on the Exemption of the Buddhist Clergy from the requirements of Civil Etiquette," in *Liebenthal Festschrift: Sino-Indian Studies* 3–4, ed. Kshitis Roy (Santiniketan: Visvabharati, 1957), p. 81.

28. Liang Qichao in "Zhongguo fofa xingshuai," p. 8, gave an estimate that in the North alone, Buddhist temples by 540 C.E. numbered 30,000 and believers reached an astonishing sum of two million.

29. For Huan's letter, see "Yu bazuo lun shamen jingshi shu 與八座論沙門敬事書," in *Hongmingji* 12: 14b. For discussions of Huan Xuan and Huiyuan, see Zürcher 1: 231–32 (where quotation of the same passage cited here contains typo in which 通 became 誦), and Kenneth Ch'en, *Transformation*, pp. 72–77.

30. *Quanli di huangyan*, pp. 125–177.

31. My translation of this difficult sentence from Huiyuan stems from considering the possibility of the monk's allusion to a passage like *Zhuangzi* 2: 35, which, in A.C. Graham's rendering, reads: "things however peculiar or incongruous, the Way interchanges them and deems them one. Their dividing is formation, their formation is dissolution; all things whether forming or dissolving in reverting interchange and are deemed to be one. Only the man who sees right through knows how to interchange and deem them one (恢恑憰怪，道通為一。其分也，成也；其成也，毀也。凡物無成與毀，復通為一。惟達者知通為一)." See *Chuang-tzŭ: the Seven Inner Chapters and Other Writings from the Book*, trans. A.C. Graham (London: Allen and Unwin, 1981), p. 53.

32. Translation, slightly modified, cited from Hurvitz, p. 99. Chinese text taken from Huiyuan, "Shamen bujing wangzhe lun," in Kimura Eiichi 木村英一, ed., *Eon Kenkyū: Ibun-hen* 慧遠研究：遺文篇 (Tokyo: Sōbunsha, 1960), p. 85.

33. *Ibid.*, p. 86. My translation.

34. For example, Reiko Ohnuma, "The Gift of the Body and the Gift of Dharma," *HR* 37/4 (May 1998): 360–400.

35. *Buddhist Conquest*, 1: 254.

36. Ch'en, *Transformation*, pp. 80–81.

37. *Ibid.*, pp. 95–97. For an informative account of how this attempt, on the part of state government, to regulate the Saṅgha and its development of the married clergy in modern Japan, see Richard M. Jaffe, *Neither Monk nor Layman: Clerical Marriage in Modern Japanese Buddhism* (Princeton: Princeton University Press, 2001), esp. chs. 1–4.

38. See *T* 54. 247b and the two translations in *T* 8. 825a–834b and *T* 8. 834a–845b. For a recent study, see Charles D. Orzech, *Politics and Transcendent Wisdom: The Scripture for Human Kings in Chinese Buddhism* (University Park: Pennsylvania State University Press, 1998).

39. *Transformation*, p. 124.

40. Gu Zhengmei, *Cong tianwang chuantong dao fowang chuantong* 從天王傳統到佛王傳統 (Taibei: Shangzhou chubanshe, 2003), p. 13.

41. Gu Zhengmei, *Guishuang fojiao zhengzhi chuantong yu Dasheng fojiao* 貴霜佛教政治傳統與大乘佛教 (Taibei: Yunchen congkan, 1993). See ch. 5, pp. 253–376 and her *Cong Tianwang chuantong*, ch. 8, pp. 377–424 for her detailed acocunt of Wu Zetian's new policies.

42. Xiao Gongquan 蕭公權, *Zhongguo zhengzhi sixiangshi* 中國政治思想史 2 vols. (Taibei: Zhongguo wenhua xueyuan, 1981), 1: 6.

43. For a definitive study of Aśoka in his Indian root and context, see John S. Strong, *The Legend of King Aśoka: A Study and Translation of the Aśokāvadāna*, Buddhist Tradition Series VI (Delhi: Motilal Banarsidass, 1989). Gu Zhengmei's resarch extrapolates Aśoka's significance and richly elaborates its impact on Chinese political developments.

44. On Daoist script and theory of language, see Isabelle Robinet, *Méditation taoïste* (Paris: Dervy-livres, 1979), chs. 1–3; English edition, *Taoist Meditation: The Mao-shan Tradition of Great Purity*, trans. Julian F. Pas and Norman J. Girardot (Albany: State University of New York Press, 1993); and Gong Pengcheng, *Daojiao xin lun*, ch. 2, pp. 39–78.

45. *Cong Tianwang chuantong*, p. 40.

46. The whole account is detailed in *Hou Hanshu* 72.

47. *Cong Tianwang chuantong*, ibid.

48. *Hou Hanshu* 60.

49. The quoted statements are all taken from the "Shi-Lao zhi 釋老志," in *Weishu* 魏書 114. See also 3/A and 3/B for the "Basic Annals of Taiwu [Shizu]," the "Biography of Cui Hao" in 35, and the "Biography of Cui Hong 崔宏 [Hao's father]," in *Beishi* 北史 21. For modern accounts, see Ch'en, *Buddhism*, pp. 147–51; Tang Yongtong 湯用彤, *Han-Wei Liang-Jin Nai-Bei chao Fojiaoshi* 漢魏兩晉南北朝佛教史 (2 vols. 1938; rpt. Taibei: Commericial Press, 1968), 2: 56–58. An important scholarly translation of the "Shi-Lao zhi" may be found in Leon Hurvitz, trans., *Treatise on Buddhism and Taoism*, An English translation of the original Chinese Text of Wei Shu CXIV and the Japanese Annotation of Tsukomoto Zenryu (Kyoto: Jimbungaku Kenkyusho, 1956).

50. *Buddhism*, p. 151.

51. "Annals of Liang 梁紀" 22, in *Zizhi tongjian* 116, 4:3642–3672.

52. Ch'en, *Buddhism*, pp. 184–86.

53. *Ibid.*, p. 187; "Shangdang Gangsuwang Huan 上黨剛肅王渙," in *Bei Qi shu* 北齊書 12; also *Guang Hongmingji* 6 in *T* 52: 124.

54. For a detailed translation of part of the memorial, see Ch'en, *Buddhism*, pp. 189–190.

55. "Wudi I 武帝上," in *Zhou shu* 周書 5.

56. See *juan* 10 in *T*. 52: 154–57.

57. *Ibid., loc. cit.*; Ch'en, *Buddhism*, p. 191.

58. *Zhou shu, loc. cit.* A more detailed reconstruction of the incidents of the debates and the circumstances surrounding the decree of proscription from other sources may be found in Tang Yongtong, 2: 90–92.

59. Ch'en, *Buddhism*, p. 192.

60. Ch'en thought them "manifestly an exaggeration," but Tang Yongtong in 2: 92 simply cited the Chinese source without comment. The source may be found in Fei Changfang 費長房, "Lidai sanbaoji 歷代三寶記," 11, in *Xuxiu Siku quanshu* 續修四庫全書 (Shanghai: Shanghai guji, 1995–2002), 1288: 580–81.

61. Ch'en, *Buddhism*, p. 232.

62. *The Ghost Festival in Medieval China* (Princeton: Princeton University Press, 1988), p. 97.

63. For Ennin's journal, see *Nittō guhō junrei kōki* 入唐求法巡禮行記, in Ono Katsutoshi 小野勝年, *Nittō guhō junrei kōki no kenkyū* 入唐求法巡禮行記の研究 (4 vols. Tokyo: Suzuki gakujutsu zaidan, 1964–69), 3. For an English version, see Edwin O. Reischauer, trans., *Ennin's Diary: The Record of a Pilgrimage to China in Search of the Law* (New York: Ronald Press, 1955). Contemporary scholarly accounts of the Huichang suppression that have made crucial use of Ennin's testimony, apart from Ch'en, include Tang Yongtong, *Sui-Tang fojiao shigao* 隋唐佛教史稿 (Beijing: Zhonghua shuju, 1982), pp. 40–51; and Stanley Weinstein, *Buddhism Under the Tang* (Cambridge: Cambridge University Press, 1987), pp. 114–136.

64. Text in *QTW* 1: 350. My translation follows the slightly different wording of the text also found in the *THY* 47 in 1: 984–85.

65. The classic here is Jacques Gernet, *Les Aspects économiques du bouddhisme dans la société chinoise du Ve au Xe siècle* (Saigon: Ecole Française d'Extrême-Orient, 1956); English edition, *Buddhism in Chinese Society: An Economic History from the Fifth to the Tenth Centuries*, trans. Franciscus Verellen (New York: Columbia University Press, 1995). See also Michael T. Dalby, "Court politics in late T'ang times," in *CHC* 5: 667.

66. See Kenneth Ch'en, "The Economic Background of the Hui-ch'ang Suppression of Buddhism," *HJAS* 19/1–2 (1956): 67–105.

67. Weinstein, p. 130, based on report by Ennin.

68. I cite Teiser's modified translation of Ennin in *Ghost Festival*, p. 98.

69. Weinstein, p. 134.

70. *Ibid.*, p. 133.

71. The standard biography is the *Da Tang Ci'ensi Sanzang Fashi zhuan* 大唐慈恩寺三藏法師傳 (hereafter cited as FSZ), collected in *Tang Xuanzang Sanzang zhuanshi huibian* 唐玄奘三藏傳史彙編, ed. Guangzhong fashi 光仲法師 (Taibei: Dongda, 1988), pp. 1–2.

72. So Arthur F. Wright, "T'ang T'ai-tsung and Buddhism," in *Perspectives on the T'ang*, eds. Arthur F. Wright and Denis Twichett (New Haven: Yale University Press, 1973), pp. 239–264.

73. Sally Hovey Wriggins, *Xuanzang, A Buddhist Pilgrim on the Silk Road* (Boulder: Westview Press, 1996), p. 3.

74. *Da Tang gu Sanzang Xuanzang Fashi xingzhuang* 大唐故三藏玄奘法師行狀, in *zhuanshi huibian*, p. 289.

75. Exhorting his appointed officials, the king in the *Classic of Documents* said: "Oh! All you virtuous officials that I have, honor your charges, and be careful with the decrees you issue. Once issued, they must be executed and not retracted. When you use that which is public (*gong* 公) to eliminate that which is personal (*si*), the people will be gladly obedient." See "Zhou guan 周官," in *Shangshu jisji* 尚書集釋, ed. Qu Wanli 屈萬里 (Taibei: Lianjing, 1983), p. 325. Although this passage is likely apocryphal and dates to the Warring States period, the injunction to "use that which is public to eliminate the private (*yi gong mie si* 以公滅私)" has become nonetheless an entrenched slogan from antiquity to the present.

76. See Yü Ying-shih 余英時, *Xiandai Ruxue lun* 現代儒學論 (River Edge: Global Publishing, 1996), chs. 1, 2, 4, 5.

77. "Fanyi wenxue yu fodian 翻譯文學與佛典," in *Foxue shiba pian*, p. 11. Although the illogic of Liang's chauvinistic remarks here seems apparent, what is obvious still merits a clear delineation. According to him, Christian and Islamic devotion betrays only superstition (*mixin* 迷信), but somehow the interest in Buddhist teachings— whether partial, partisan, or of the whole tradition—is to be characterized as scholarly and intellectual. Whether Liang's attitude reflects the famous but ill-defined spirit of May Fourth is not my concern here. It is its persistence down to the present among a sizeable segment of Chinese savants worldwide that bestows on the serious study of Chinese religions a special burden.

78. See Jacques Gernet, *Buddhism in Chinese Society*, pp. xiii–xvii.

1. Overmyer, "Attitudes," 192.

2. *The Republic of China Yearbook* (Taipei: Government Information Office, 1999), p. 679.

3. Prasenjit Duara, *Rescuing History from the Nation: Questioning Narratives of Modern China* (Chicago: University of Chicago Press, 1995), pp. 95–110.

4. Prasenjit Duara, *Sovereignty and Authenticity: Manchukuo and the East Asian Modern* (Lanham: Rowman and Littlefield, 2003), pp. 109–122.

5. *Ibid.*, pp. 103–07.

6. Charles Brewer Jones, *Buddhism in Taiwan: Religion and the State, 1660–1990* (Honolulu: University of Hawaii Press, 1999); Paul R. Katz, "Religion and the State in Post-war Taiwan," *CQ* 174 (June 2003): 395–412; and *Religion in Modern Taiwan: Tradition and Innovation in a Changing Society*, eds. Philip Clart and Charles B. Jones (Honolulu: University of Hawaii Press, 2003).

7. See the most informative discussion in Pitman B. Potter, "Belief in Control: Regulation of Religion in China," *CQ* 174 (June 2003): 317–337.

8. Potter, in *ibid.*, 325, citing Constitution of 1982 published by Beijing's Publishing House of Law, 1986.

9. See above, Chapter 1, footnote 4.

10. See Holmes Welch, *Buddhism under Mao* (Cambridge, Massachusetts: Harvard University Press, 1972).

11. Lai Chi-Tim, "Daoism in China Today, 1980–2002," *CQ* 174 (June 2003): 413–427.

12. Raoul Birnbaum, "Buddhist China at the Century's Turn," *CQ* 174 (June 2003): 428–450.

13. These poignant words are those of Elizabeth Sifton, daughter of the late Reinhold Niebuhr, renowned American theologian living in the first half of the twentieth century. The words were cited in Ann Hulbert's review of Sifton's book, *The Serenity Prayer: Faith and Politics* (New York: Norton, 2003) in the *New York Times Book Review* (November 2nd, 2003), p. 12.

14. *New York Times* (April 16th, 2003), p. A3.

15. *New York Times* (October 1st, 2003), p. A4.

16. *New York Times* (October 27th, 2003), p. A4.

17. See "Le rapport de la commission Stasi sur la laïcité," special supplement to *Le Monde* (12 Décembre 2003), p. 1.1 "Un principe républicain construit par l'histoire."

18. *New York Times* (December 12th, 2003).

19. *New York Times* (February 26th, 2004), pp. A1, A18.

20. See the sobering and devastating study by Bruce Lincoln, *Holy Terrors: Thinking about Religion after September 11* (Chicago: University of Chicago Press, 2003).

21. See the *New York Times* (February 20th, 2004), p. A4.

22. Wechsler, *Offerings of Jade and Silk*, p. 123, citing the scholarship of Victor Turner and Abner Cohen.

23. *Hanshu*, 73, 10: 3116.

INDEX

CPSIA information can be obtained
at www.ICGtesting.com
Printed in the USA
LVOW11s0819310117
522717LV00002B/14/P